THE INCUMBENT
TEA PARTY

The Incumbent
Tea Party

Dale Young

iUniverse, Inc.
Bloomington

The Incumbent Tea Party

iUniverse books may be ordered through booksellers or by contacting:

iUniverse
1663 Liberty Drive
Bloomington, IN 47403
www.iuniverse.com
1-800-Authors (1-800-288-4677)

ISBN: 978-1-4620-2444-5 (sc)
ISBN: 978-1-4620-1339-5 (hc)
ISBN: 978-1-4620-1338-8 (ebk)

Printed in the United States of America

iUniverse rev. date: 08/23/2011

CONTENTS

This book is being written because, as a normal citizen of these great United States, I have come to the conclusion that something has to be done to put us back on the track that our forefathers put us on.

If you look at the Constitution that started this great country, you will see that a lot of what is happening was not intended. The federal government has gotten way too large and entirely out of control. This country is doing things that our forefathers never intended it to do. The people who supposedly represent "we the people" no longer represent us but the special interests. It has gotten so the incumbent will always get reelected in every part of the country.

I truly believe that this is the reason that we as Americans have come to loathe the voting process. You always hear people say, "Why should I vote? It doesn't make a difference." I say it will only make a difference if we the people stand up and make our voices heard.

Have you ever wondered why you always hear the politicians talking about social security and Medicare? Have you ever wondered why they are always talking about the items that don't really relate to the things you feel are important in your life? Well, that is due to the senior citizens being a constant voting bloc. In any given election you will only see about 50 percent of the American public vote. Now about a quarter of these are senior citizens; the others are evenly divided between left-wing nuts, far-right nuts, and finally, the political junkies like me who follow politics as if our lives depended on it, which of course they do.

But just think about it. You have a lot of crazy people out there directing which way this country should go. And it all depends on which side gets the most nuts to come out and vote for their side. For the last election we had about a 60 percent turnout, which was great. And I truly believe that a lot of normal, average Americans came out. They are the true heart of this great country, the ones who make the wheels turn. They are the ones who get up in the morning even though they would rather stay in bed and dream about what this country could be, what this country has been.

This is the great country that against all odds turned the redcoats away, stopped the horrible and not-soon-forgotten Hitler. This is the great country that stopped the Japanese from taking over after our military was decimated at Pearl Harbor. Did we give up and say, "Oh well, we don't have a chance in hell after this"? No, we got our asses out of bed in the morning, rolled up our sleeves, and changed everything we did to stop them. It was our heart that stopped them.

This is the country that lived through the Great Depression. When times were hell, and jobs were very few and far between, did we give up and say, "Oh well, life's a bitch; let's just quit"? No, we stood tall and helped each other out. We picked up that guy off the street who felt he had nothing else to live for and gave him a reason to press on.

I think that we are at our best when the chips are down. That is when we stand up and cheer for the little guy. We cheer for hope, and last but not least, we cheer for freedom. I think this is what makes us different from every other country on this earth. When times get tough, when it seems the end is near, we look at ourselves in the mirror and say, "No matter what happens or what this day brings, I am free. I am free to create my own destiny." What other people in this world can truly say that and mean it?

In this book I am going to try and convey what I feel will truly bring a change to our country. I feel that the only way to bring about change is to vote out the incumbents. Yes, you have it right: vote out the career politicians. Now we are not going to do this the way I'm sure everyone is thinking. We are not going to change our voting habits. If you are a Republican, you are not going to vote for a Democrat, nor will Democrats vote Republican. I think everyone knows that I could never make that happen. This is because all Americans are set in their own habits, which I would never pretend to think I could change.

You have to realize that there's no need to vote against your own political beliefs. All you have to do is vote for the other Republican or the other Democrat. Yes, you heard me right, just vote for the other guy.

Most Americans never come out to vote unless it is in a general election. On average about 40 percent of the American public comes out to vote in a general election, and that's in a presidential year. What we need to do is come out during the primaries. Come out and vote during the time we are expected to vote on which Republican or Democrat will run during the general election. If we the people stand up and voice our support for the other guy, I am sure we all will see change in the way this country is run.

In the following chapters, I will show reason after reason why I feel this is our only option. Just look back at the '94 elections, when the Republicans took over the House and Senate. You can see how much things got done during that time. It may have only lasted a few short years, but I think you can plainly see how it changed the mind-set in Washington. The elected politicians woke up and started paying attention to the American people and not the special interest groups—at least until they realized that we were back to sleep in our warm comfortable beds, the same beds which they in Washington made for us. We were over our temper tantrum, and they could return to their back-room deals and their Friday night poker games where they bet our entire future on a straight flush, neither knowing nor caring that the other side had a full house.

If we the people don't wake up, we will soon find ourselves looking out the front door asking ourselves why we didn't see it coming. Oh, we saw it, but we were too interested in getting that BMW or that plasma TV. We keep telling ourselves that there is nothing we can do; they will just keep doing what they want. That is only because we have been Rip van Winkle and asleep for the past twenty years. Or is it thirty or forty or even fifty years?

We the people are the only ones who will ever make a difference. The good old boys and girls in Washington are only interested in where their next free meal will come from. When this great country started, the job of a congressman or senator was a part-time job. Now it's an extra-innings baseball game where there will be no winners.

Have you ever watched them have sessions that go late into the night? Do you think this is because they are devoted to their job and want only the best for us? No, they are there late into the night when most Americans are sound asleep because they don't want us to know what they are passing. That is when most reporters will not want to stay up and keep watch over them. That's when they sneak in those little unknown amendments. You ask any politician if he or she ever read an entire bill that he or she voted on and I bet you he or she will say no. How many politicians ever read the Patriot Act before it was signed?

So here we go. Hopefully little old me can change just a little bit of what goes on in Washington. But I cannot do any of this without the help of each and every American living today. This can only be done if we stand together to change the way things happen in this great country. As the old saying goes, together we stand and divided we fall. I just hope we end up on the same side.

CHAPTER 2

US AGAINST THEM

We as Americans need to wake up and smell the coffee. The politicians in Washington have gotten us so wrapped around their fingers, it is ridiculous. They keep us fighting amongst ourselves so much that we are too busy to really see what they are doing. Whether it's the blacks versus the whites, pro-life versus pro-choice, old versus young, Republican versus Democrat—you can put any name you want on it, and the outcome is the same: us versus ourselves instead of us versus them.

One of the biggest ways that they do this is the old black-versus-white battle. Now you and I both know that there will always be stupid idiots who don't like blacks, just like there will be stupid idiots who don't like whites. It is always the same; all you have to do is substitute white or black with Jews or Catholics. We will never get rid of these idiots. They usually sink their own boats anyway. Overall, I feel that the whites in this country do not have any animosity against African Americans. Hey, by the way who do you think created the word African American anyway? Yes, you got that right, the politicians. Why do we have to be broken down into subcategories? Asian American, African American, Irish American? Why can't we all just be Americans? Because the politicians want us to keep looking at each other as a subcategory. After 9/11 I bet we—no, I know that we—were all just plain old Americans.

I truly feel that we as Americans are too busy trying to keep our heads above water to be worrying about what the white or black man is doing. I truly believe that the majority of Americans, both white and black, want the best for every American regardless of their color or nationality. However, as long as the politicians keep us fighting against each other, we will not see what they are doing. That is their little way of staying in power, and, trust me, it is all about the power when you get down to it.

Do you remember right after the attacks of September 11, 2001? We as Americans came together for a cause. Can you look back on that day and remember those pictures on TV of the New Yorkers and other people from around the world running from the World Trade Center? The sight of the victims covered completely in the dust of death that surrounded that day? Everyone looked the same that day. You could not tell who was white, who was black, who was Irish; you could not tell one person from the next. Everyone's skin was the same color. Can you picture that in your mind? It will definitely not leave my mind anytime soon.

Well, we as Americans need to wake up and go back to that day. Not to the violence that caused it, but the unity that it created. For a few months we all forgot about our petty differences. For a blink of an eye, we were as one. Even in Washington they all came together; even the world if only for a moment. Why can't we get back to that moment? It used to be a person running for office in this country did it to change America. And I believe that there are still people elected to office that strive for just that.

Whatever happened to what President Kennedy said: "Ask not what your country can do for you. Ask what you can do for your country"? I think those are some of the most important words ever spoken by one of our great presidents. Because I believe that is what our founding fathers truly meant to happen when they created this great country.

When are we as Americans going to stop looking to the government to solve our problems? When are we going to reach deep down inside ourselves and reach that level of understanding that it wasn't the government that has kept this great country going over the last 230-some years, It was the American people. Yes, you and I, with our dreams of being what we thought we could become. It was each of us reaching that plateau; it was Martin Luther King believing that a man should be judged by the content of his character rather than the color of his skin. Dr. King could have accepted that blacks were second-class citizens, but no, he knew better. In addition, because of the dreams of one great man, this country is a whole lot better off, and we are a much wiser country. It sometimes takes great men like him to make us believe in ourselves. Yes, believe that each one of us has a dream.

Moreover, as long as we bust our butts and work hard and never give up, we can achieve that dream and any other that happens to pop up in our heads. We can reach the top of every mountain that we attempt to climb. All we have to do is keep putting one foot in front of the other and keep telling ourselves we will make it—even when our muscles start to ache, when we think we cannot go any farther. It is important that we look up at the top of each mountain and say, "I am not going to quit." Because any dream worth dreaming, worth fighting for, is going to have rocks on the path. Some are small and some are large, some may seem impossible to get around. However, you must never give up, because when you reach the top of the mountain, then and only then will you know the heart and soul of this great country.

One way to get up that mountain and ensure realizing your dream is to get out of the way of all the people who have given up. If you surround yourself with all the people who have given up, then you will be putting their burdens upon your shoulders too. They will keep tugging on your shirt, holding you down, taking your mind off the goal . . . they will just slow you down.

In a sense, this is what the politicians are doing to all of us. They keep us so involved in our petty differences that we never look to see what they are doing. They know that the average voter is going to vote the same way every time. That is why every ten years they redistrict each area to benefit whoever is in power. They have got us controlled like mice in a laboratory experiment. They control us by telling us what the important issue of the day is. Why is it that, in the last California election, not one state house or senate seat changed hands? Is it because Californians are so happy with the way things are going there? You tell me, all you voters in California. I guess you are so happy that you just recalled your governor a little while back.

We are so brainwashed into voting one way or another that we do not see what is happening. Ask yourself this: how many of us vote Democrat or Republican only because that is, how our parents voted? How many of us truly research the issues before we go in the voting booth?

This is why it is so important to vote out the incumbent. If for just one election, we all go out during the primaries and vote for the other guy, if we replace the majority of the House and Senate with new people, this would most likely raise a few eyebrows in Washington. Wouldn't the politicians in your state be pulling their hair out trying to figure out what happened? In addition, the few that were still there would most likely start singing another tune.

That is why we need to do this so we can once again put this great country back on the road our forefathers put it on. We need to show all those politicians that it is we the people who are the United States of America and not them. We need to stop them from using us against each other just to line their pockets with all the money from special interest groups. Just like the Boston Tea Party, we need to have an Incumbent Tea Party. I truly believe this can happen, I truly believe we can take back this great country of ours.

Why is it that in the last twenty years, 90 percent of the African Americans voted Democratic and 90 percent of the pro-lifers voted Republican? Are you better off? Ask yourself that. No, because we are so scared to change anything in our lives. We as Americans are a funny bunch. We are so wrapped up in our daily routines, and we are in no way going to change that. We are creatures of habit, and once they get us in that cycle, they have us. And trust me when I say they know exactly what they are doing. We as Americans have to be willing to change the way we do things before we will ever see any kind of change in Washington.

Remember the change that happened when Reagan was voted in as our president back in 1980? If you had told someone in 1980 that the Cold War would be won without a single shot being fired . . . let us just say that you most likely would have ended up in the crazy house. However, because a great man had an idea to do something different than all the other presidents, things changed and for the better. And, yes, I believe there is yet another great man or great woman out there waiting to step up to the plate and hit another home run.

Do not let them control you anymore. Decide today that the next election, the next time you go to the polls, you are going to send that message. You are going to vote out the incumbent, and you are going to vote into office that other person. Only you and the rest of America together can truly make a difference. Only you and America together can make a change in this great country of ours.

CHAPTER 3

SOCIAL SECURITY

"Social security." Don't you just love the sound of that phrase? That word *security* makes you feel so warm and fuzzy. Just knowing that you don't have to do anything throughout your life to ensure that, when you retire, you are covered. "The government is going to take care of me."

Yes, that's right: when you turn sixty-five, your government is going to take care of you. Thank you, Uncle Sam. Yes, the politicians made up that term so we would see the government as family. And you know you can always trust family. You ever wonder why the senior citizens are the biggest voting bloc in America? It's because we have become so dependent on the government that we have no other choice. If you don't believe me, ask Lesko. I'm sure he will explain all the government programs to you for only two payments of $29.95 plus shipping and handling.

I think the reason he wears all those question marks on his clothes is that he wants to ask how the hell we ever got to this point in America. How did we get to where, instead of looking inside ourselves for the answers, we all look to the government? I know that we as Americans don't go through our entire lives wanting to depend on Uncle Sam. Nevertheless, the politicians have gotten us there. When are they going to do what's best for the country instead of what's best for the state?

Yes, the politicians have taken us to that point. Remember when it only took one person in a family to work to take care of that family? Now if both parents are not working, we can't survive. Why is that, I ask you? Think about it, it takes both parents to work just to pay all the taxes to support the gigantic government that has taken control of every one of us. They tell us that it's women's rights, and in some small way they may be right about that. However, I think once they saw how much money was rolling into the treasury, they couldn't control themselves. They were just giddy about all the money rolling in, and, of course, they kept finding ways to bring in more. They found new ways to pit us against each other, as I stated in the last chapter. Yes, they created the glass ceiling, and they were sure to clean the glass every day.

When did we in America start to give up on ourselves and start giving all hope to Uncle Sam? When and why did we ever sell our souls to the government? Why is it we no longer have any faith in ourselves.

Do you remember the Constitution?

> We the people of the United States, in order to form a more perfect union, establish justice, insure domestic Tranquility, provide for the common defense, promote the general welfare, and secure the blessings of Liberty to ourselves and our posterity, do ordain and establish this constitution for the United States of America.

That is one of the greatest papers ever written on this earth. Where does it say that we are to give up and pass everything over to the government? It doesn't say that anywhere in that document. In fact, it is very specific in what powers the government has.

Nevertheless, we as Americans have slowly shifted the responsibility and given Uncle Sam control of our lives. We keep listening to the politicians about how we can't take care of ourselves. Yes, we need Uncle Sam to take care of us. Why are we not able to take care of ourselves, to save for our own retirement? If you took away even half the taxes that you have given to Uncle Sam throughout your life, you would be amazed at what the amount comes up to. In addition, even if you still fell on hard times, why is it not possible for the kids to take care of Mom and Dad? Think of all the things that Mom and Dad did for us when we were young and stupid. Think of all your bad decisions as an eighteen-to-twenty-one-year-old. Yes, they bailed you out without even thinking about it. So why can't you as an adult take a little pressure off their shoulders? The only reason they are dependent on the government is that they don't want to be a burden to you.

Well, you answer this question: are they a burden? Why is it that you cannot be there for them so they don't have to look to Uncle Sam? It must be that your BMW and your big-screen television are much more important to you than your parents. There is one way to be sure that your kids will be there for you, and that is if they see you taking care of Grandma and Grandpa. You have to be the one who shows them that nothing in this world matters more than family. If you can't depend on family, then whom can you truly depend on?

We have to get away from being so materialistic in this world. We have gotten so that all that matters is that BMW, that plasma TV, that fifty-six-inch barbecue grill. In addition, that has translated into "I need that Nintendo or X-box." If these are truly the things that are important in our lives, is it any wonder that these are the priorities we are passing on to our kids?

Moreover, if we keep this up you will find out where this will lead. When you are laid up in an old folks' home, paid for of course by the government, and your kids show up to visit maybe once or twice a month if you're lucky, you will ask yourself, "Where did I go wrong? Why are they treating me this way?" That's because the government is taking care of you. Why should your kids take care of you when Uncle Sam is there? He is the next best thing to family, right? It doesn't matter that you have bedsores; it doesn't matter that the person wiping your butt could not care less about you. That's right, have no fear, Uncle Sam is here to save the day.

One of the most important times in my life was when my mom was dying of breast cancer. I spent the last two months of her life, with the help of the family, taking care of her. I cannot tell you the stress that we went through during that time. Some of you know just what I'm talking about. That's what I thought then; now I deeply cherish those last two months of her life. I would not give them up for anything in the world—those late nights at the hospice house and eventually the last few nights at my sister's house, those talks through the wee hours about life and what it means.

I saw those workers at the hospice house care for her. They showed me what being American is all about: the sacrifices those nurses make, the hardships that they have to endure every day of their life, the way they continue to do their job each day even though someone close to them is on their way out of this world. Most of us will never be able to comprehend what they endure day in and day out. Can you imagine meeting people every day, knowing that within the next two weeks they most likely will no longer be around? Once again, I would not give up those last two months for anything in this world.

In addition, I am a better person because of it. Those moments are ingrained within my mind forever. If I had depended on the government to take care of her, I would have missed all of that. Those last few moments with Mom made me realize that life is too short. We never know when the good Lord is going to call us home. I truly believe God gave us life, but I also believe He gave us death to show us that we should take nothing for granted, that we must live each day as if there were no tomorrow.

When we are young, we think we have our whole life ahead of us. However, as we get older and the friends and loved ones around us start leaving this earth, we start to think about just how much time we truly have left. That is why it is so important to teach our kids that above all else family is number one. We cannot depend on the government to take care of our family. We must make it a priority to ensure we are the ones to do it. Even though at the time you will have to endure the sadness and the pain, believe it when I say you will never regret it; on the contrary, you will cherish those moments. You will forever remember those late-night conversations about life and love, and what not to forget in life. They are the most truthful and unforgettable times you will ever spend with your loved ones.

So please, let's not let our future generation be dependent on Uncle Sam. Let's strive for a day when the senior citizens of this country are a major voting bloc for their grandchildren and the future of this country. Let's hope that the last thing they have to worry about is whether their kids or grandkids are going to be there for them. Let's hope that the last thing on their mind is whether their Statue of Liberty check will show up on the first of the month.

Let's all pray that the politicians won't be able to use your grandparents as a political ploy; that they won't be able to say, "Why does Grandma have to choose between eating dinner or buying that medicine?" I would think that we as Americans are caring enough to help out Grandma and buy that medicine for her. If she could depend on her family, then she would not have to depend on Uncle Sam. In addition, you would get to spend the same lasting memorable time that I got to spend with my mom. I can only pray that you end up with the same great memories.

In addition, even if the kids are not still around, then there are many other places for us to find help, like charities, churches, and many other organizations. How many of you do not donate to charity because you know Uncle Sam is there to foot the bill? However, how many of you realize that only about 30 or 40 percent of that dollar goes to help those people out? How many people actually realize that your employer matches the amount of money that you pay into Uncle Sam. Look at your pay stub and think about the amount of money that is going to Uncle Sam.

Now I tell you again, we together need to go out during the next election and throw out the incumbents. This is the only way we are going to get those politicians in Washington to open up their eyes and start to do what's best for the country and not what's best for them.

The following came to me as an e-mail. I don't know who started it, but he or she sure did come up with a good idea.

Social Security 2009 (Author Unknown)

Let us show our leaders in Washington "people power" and the power of the [[missing word??]]

It doesn't matter if you are REPUBLICAN or DEMOCRAT!

Propose this in 2009: Start a bill to place all politicians on social security:

(This is worth reading. It is short and to the point.)

Perhaps we are asking the wrong questions during election years.

Our senators and congresswomen do not pay into social security and, of course, they do not collect from it. You see, social security benefits were not suitable for persons of their rare elevation in society. They felt they should have a special plan for themselves. So, many years ago they voted in their own benefit plan.

In more recent years, no congressperson has felt the need to change it. After all, it is a great plan. For all practical purposes their plan works like this:

When they retire, they continue to draw the same pay until they die. Except it may increase from time to time for cost of living adjustments . . .

For example, Senator Byrd and Congressman White and their wives may expect to draw $7,800,000.00 (that's seven million eight hundred thousand dollars), with their wives drawing $275,000.00 during the last years of their lives. This is calculated on an average life span for each of those two dignitaries.

Younger dignitaries who retire at an early age, will receive much more during the rest of their lives.

Their cost for this excellent plan is $0.00. Nada! Zilch!

This little perk they voted for themselves is free to them. You and I pick up the tab for this plan. The funds for this fine retirement plan come directly from the General Funds, "our tax dollars at work"!

From our own social security plan, which you and I pay (or have paid) into, every payday until we retire (which amount is matched by our employer), We can expect to get an average of $1,000 per month after retirement.

Or, in other words, we would have to collect our average of $1,000 monthly benefits for 68 years and one (1) month to equal Senator Bill Bradley's benefits!

Social security could be very good if only one small change were made. That change would be to jerk the Golden Fleece Retirement Plan from under the senators and congressmen. Put them into the social security plan with the rest of us. Then sit back . . . and see how fast they would fix it!

If enough people receive this, maybe a seed of awareness will be planted and maybe good changes will evolve.

How many people can <u>YOU</u> send this to?

Better yet . . . How many people <u>WILL</u> you send this to?

CHAPTER 4

FEES AND TAXES:
WHAT'S THE DIFFERENCE?

You have to give kudos to the politicians. They have created a perfect world within the world of government. Once they found out that the word *tax* was a four-letter word, they then came up with the word *fee*. This, by the way, is also a four-letter word.

However, once again we are so involved with our own lives that we cannot tell the difference. This is because we see the word *fee*, and we think that it is the company that is charging us that fee. Besides, it is only forty-nine cents, and that is not much to ask to help the kids. Yes, that is usually their excuse. They love using the phrase "It's for the kids."

Here let us look at just a couple of the fees that show up on our bills. Go ahead and pull out your bills. Electric, phone, cable, gas—they are all the same. They are all full of taxes and fees pushed on us, capped off by some unknown surcharge or service fee. However, no matter what they call them, they are all the same in my opinion: *taxes*. They have gotten us so wrapped up in our day-to-day routines that we do not pay attention. Moreover, just as Ronald Reagan once said, "There is nothing so permanent as a government program," you can say the same thing about a government tax or fee. Let's look at some monthly bills.

PHONE BILL

Monthly Service

Resident flat rate service	$10.69
TOTAL MONTHLY SERVICE	$10.69

FEES AND TAXES

Federal Subscriber line charge	$ 4.49
Number Portability Svc Charge	$ .34
9-1-1 Emergency System	$ .08
CA High cost fund Surcharge-A	$ .02
CA High cost fund Surcharge-B	$ .29
Universal Lifeline Telephone Service Surcharge	$ .13
Rate surcharge	$(.14) CR
State Regulatory Fee	$ .01
CA Relay Service and communication devices fund	$ .01
Federal Universal Service Fee	$ .44
Federal taxes at 3.00%	$ .50

**TOTAL LOCAL, STATE, AND FEDERAL
FEES AND TAX CHARGES** **$ 6.17**

TOTAL PHONE BILL **$16.86**

PERCENTAGE OF BILL THAT IS CHARGES	63%
PERCENTAGE OF BILL THATH IS TAXES OR FEES	**37%**

Now this is the first bill that we have looked at, and as you can see, there is a 37 percent tax on just this bill. In addition, it does not matter whether you are rich or poor; you have to pay it.

However, what they do is make the business the bad guy. That is why you always hear people putting down big business. Well, let me tell you it's not big business that is the bad guy, it's the politicians. It is just that they have their scheme down pat. You have to look at the percentage and not the dollar value. This is how pennies can add up. Let's just look at some others before we continue.

CABLE PHONE BILL

Monthly Charges

BASIC MONTHLY SERVICE	$ 9.99
TOTAL MONTHLY SERVICE	$ 9.99

FEES AND TAXES

FCC ACCESS CHARGE	$ 4.42
FEDERAL TAX	$ .68
CA RELAY SVC AND COMM DEVICE FUND	$ .05
CA HIGH COST FUND SURCHARGE A	$ .03
CA HIGH COST FUND SURCHARGE B	$ .39
TELECOM FUND	$ .03
E911 TAX	$ .13
UNIVERSAL LIFELINE SERVICE CHARGE	$ .20
STATE REGULATORY FEE	$ .02
UNIVERSAL SERVICE FUND	$ .53

TOTAL LOCAL, STATE, AND FEDERAL FEES AND TAX CHARGES $ 6.48

PHONE BILL TOTAL   **$16.47**

PERCENTAGE OF BILL THAT IS CHARGES	61%
PERCENTAGE OF BILL THAT IS TAXES OR FEES	**39%**

CABLE BILL

MONTHLY CHARGES

BASIC CABLE SERVICE	$ 8.10
TOTAL MONTHLY SERVICE	$ 8.10

FEES AND TAXES

FCC FEE	$ .03
FRANCHISE FEE	$ 2.28
TOTAL LOCAL, STATE AND FEDERAL FEES AND TAX CHARGES	$ 2.31

CABLE BILL TOTAL	**$10.41**

PERCENTAGE OF BILL THAT IS CHARGES	78%
PERCENTAGE OF BILL, THAT IS TAXES OR FEES	**22%**

AT&T WIRELESS CELL PHONE

MONTHLY CHARGES

NATIONAL PLAN	$39.99
FAMILY PLAN (ADD A PHONE)	$19.99
FAMILY MEMBER CREDIT $(10.00)	
TOTAL MONTHLY CHARGE	$49.98

**FEES AND TAXES
(THE FOLLOWING TAXES AND FEES ARE LISTED BY PHONE DUE TO MY ADDING ON A EXTRA PHONE FOR**

MY FAMILY PLAN) IN ADDITION THEY CHARGE BOTH LINES THE TAXES AND FEES.

	PHONE #1	PHONE #2
REGULATORY PROGRAMS FEE	$ 1.75	$ 1.75
UNIVERSAL CONNECTIVITY CHARGE	$ .36	$ 1.27
CALIFORNIA PUBLIC UTILITY FEE	$ .01	$ .04
STATE E911 TAX	$ .08	$ .29
UNIV LIFELINE SVC SURCHARGE	$ .09	$ .32
TELECONNECT FUND	$ .02	$ .06
RELAY SERVICE SURCHARGE	$ .02	$ .09
HIGH COST FUND A SURCHARGE	$ .01	$ .05
HIGH COST FUND B SURCHARGE	$ .21	$ .73
FEDERAL TAX	$ .37	$1.33
TOTAL TAXES AND FEES PER PHONE	**$2.92**	**$5.93**

TOTAL LOCAL, STATE, AND FEDERAL FEES AND TAX CHARGES $8.85

CELL BILL TOTAL $58.83

PERCENTAGE OF BILL THAT IS CHARGES   **85%**
PERCENTAGE OF BILL, THAT IS TAXES OR FEES   **15%**

ELECTRICITY BILL

MONTHLY CHARGES

DWR GENERATION	$13.82
SCE GENERATION	$ 9.24
DISTRIBUTION CHARGES	$45.66
TOTAL MONTHLY CHARGES	$68.72

Dale Young

FEES AND TAXES

DWR BOND CHARGE	$ 2.97
TRANSMISSION CHARGE	$ 2.67
NUCLEAR DECOMMISSIONING CHARGE	$.43
PUBLIC PURPOSE PROGRAM CHARGES	$2.66
TRUST TRANSFER AMOUNT	$5.12
OTHER TAXES	$.19

**TOTAL LOCAL, STATE, AND FEDERAL
FEES AND TAX CHARGES** $14.04

ELECTRICITY BILL TOTAL $82.76

PERCENTAGE OF BILL THAT IS CHARGES	83%

**PERCENTAGE OF BILL THAT IS
TAXES OR FEES** 17%

**TOTAL PERCENTAGE OF BILLS WHICH
ARE CHARGES** 83%
**TOTAL PERCENTAGE OF BILLS THAT IS
TAXES OR FEES** 17%

PERCENTAGES OF BILLS THAT IS FEES OR TAXES

SBC PHONE	**37%**
CABLE PHONE	**39%**
CABLE BILL	**22%**
ELECTRIC BILL	**17%**
CELL PHONE	**5%**

Go ahead and look at your bills in your home. You will find them. Go ahead, add them up, and see what percentage you are paying. Now, of course, I live in the great state of California, and we are likely the most liberal state in America besides New York. Moreover, you know what they say: Everything starts in California. Any idea that the politicians have thought up they started as a test case in California. Therefore, yours may not be as high as mine.

However, you just look out. Uncle Sam is looking forward to doing the sleight-of-hand trick in your state too. It will be just a matter of time before all these feel-good fees and taxes hit your mailbox. Once again the government keeps these taxes going, and whether you like it or not, they raise them every time they need more funds to pay off all the special interests that have donated to their cause. Whenever they need more money, you will see them working late into the night while everyone is sleeping, when no one is watching them, and they throw these fee's into an important bill like homeland security. These politicians make lawyers look like preschool kids when it comes to the small print. In addition, most of the bills they vote on are not even read by most of them.

Nevertheless, the main thing about all these fees is that they are shoved down to the business level. Of course, this means that the business has to collect and distribute them to some government agency. So, of course, they have to hire someone, or, in the case of a big company, they have to hire a group of people to track and control these funds. What this all does is bog down business with unnecessary regulations and paperwork. In addition, guess where all the money comes from to pay for all this? They raise prices on us, the consumer, or they cut back on those pay raises because they can only raise prices so much. Most of the time, it's your pay raise that is affected. However, you get mad at the boss and scream and yell about how you are not appreciated.

Well, it is about time that we as Americans start putting the blame where it belongs: right in the hands of the politicians who control our lives with all these fees. I think by now we should be able to see that getting the government out of the way and getting rid of these government fees will only bring down the price of doing business with the company you are paying the taxes to.

When have any of us ever known any business that is run by the government, whether state or federal, to be efficient? Ask yourself, is the DMV proficient? Is the post office proficient? Just ask yourself if any government agency that you have ever had to deal with is proficient.

Anything that the government is doing can be done much better by a private agency. This is because private agencies have an incentive to make the customer happy. Remember the cable company before there were satellite dishes around? It used to be they would show up sometime during the day to fix your problem. Now they give us a two-hour time window. What do you think would happen if you could get your driver's license from a private company? If those people working at the DMV had to worry about their jobs, I think they would be a whole lot more willing to help you out and at a much faster pace.

Why do you figure it is that only 40 percent of the money you send into the politicians for social security gets back to the people? If your local charity gave back to the needy only forty cents of every dollar it took in, don't you think you would be screaming bloody murder? I bet you would not be giving to that charity next time. Not to mention that your employer matches every cent that you send into social security, dollar for dollar. You would think that they would set this money aside and use it for what it was meant for. But once again we the American people were snookered. When social security started, they just told us what we wanted to hear. And because of the Great Depression, we were vulnerable. Yes, that's what they do. When we have our guard down and we are worrying about all kinds of other things, they stab us in the back.

Why is it that when the liberals controlled Washington, there was a social security crisis that they wanted to fix? Of course their solution was to raise taxes. And now when the Republicans control Washington, their idea is to give us our own accounts which we can leave to our heirs. Now the Democrats are saying there is no crisis. You would think that if it was a crisis in the '90s it would still be a crisis. But of course they don't want the Republicans to take credit for fixing the problem. And if fixing it means giving us more control over our money, then you know they don't want that to happen. Can you believe a politician actually said that that social security is solvent for another thirty years with 70 or 80 percent of the payments we were promised? Talk about out of touch. So they are willing to just wait because we the people will still get 70 or 80 percent of our own money.

CHAPTER 5

UNIONS: WHAT GIVES?

You know, when unions were first established I'm sure they were needed. Furthermore, I'm sure under certain circumstances today they still are. Those small unions in those small towns across America where their intentions are only good. Where they are looking out for the little guy or gal just like they were when they started way back when.

But I truly believe that the large unions are part of what's destroying the America we all love and adore. Why is it that a grocery store checkout clerk can make around seventeen dollars an hour? Not to mention that they also can get full health benefits, which just adds on to the pay.

Now I understand that, to Joe Six-Pack, this is great, because he is the guy getting the 17 bucks an hour. What a lot of people don't understand is that if Joe Six-Pack is getting seventeen bucks an hour, the employer is most likely paying him around thirty to thirty-five dollars an hour after you figure in the health care and the social security payments the employer pays (yes, whatever amount you are paying into social security, your employer matches it), not to mention worker's compensation insurance, and let's not forget Medicaid. And, of course, we can't forget about all those paid holidays that each employer pays for every year.

Now I'm sure we are all saying, "So what? The employer is the one paying it." Well, guess again; where do you think the employer gets all this money from? Yes, you guessed it right, by raising prices on goods. The only thing though is that they can only raise the prices so much because of the competition. Plus there is only so much you and I will pay for a loaf of bread.

Well, guess what: this just means that they hold off on hiring that new person they think they need and just make you work that much harder. And, of course, when you get that little old 2 percent pay raise at the beginning of the year, you can think about it. Explain to me why it should cost someone around thirty dollars an hour to employ a checkout clerk at the grocery store. Explain to me why they should even get seventeen bucks an hour. When I was growing up and I worked in one of the stores, I can tell you I didn't make that much. Besides, I didn't expect to. I saw that job as a steppingstone in the workplace. That is where I went to learn about being a responsible person. Please tell me what college offers a degree in running a cash register.

You know we have to wake up and see how the unions are destroying the states and companies that they are involved in and quite possibly this country. Why is it that when you apply for a job and you want to work for a certain company that is unionized, you must join the union, where you are required to pay union dues, even though you may not believe in the union?

One of the biggest downfalls of being unionized, from the business's point of view, is that when you have to lay people off, you must lay off the junior person on the payroll first, not the least productive. This is the way it works: if you have a salesperson who is bringing in two million dollars in sales a year for your company, and you have another that is only bringing in one million dollars, but he is more senior, then you must lay off the more productive person. Now tell me if you were running this company, who would you lay off? I truly don't know why these companies allow this to happen; maybe they are like Congress and never read the union contracts.

Now this involves a domino effect: by laying off the least productive, your company just lost a million in sales. But if you had laid off the other guy this would have allowed you to break even. You may have been able to keep a few more folks employed, but instead you have to lay more people off; of course they are the junior employees. The dominoes keep falling, and it just continues to be one vicious cycle. And all this time the management for the union doesn't really care because they are still pulling in their six-figure incomes.

The reason I think the unions are allowed to keep this up is that the unions are in the back pocket of the Democratic Party. And these companies are afraid to go against the government. It's like a mafia racket. If you go into any Democratic-controlled state, including my great state of California, you will find that the majority of the business done in the state for the state contracts must be done by unions; otherwise, you must pay the prevailing wage. And, of course, that is a code word for union wages.

That's why you have men or women working on road crews holding stop signs and controlling traffic, who are making $40.42 an hour; at least that's the wage here in California. And as they say, as California goes, so goes the nation. Let's think about this: we are paying someone forty dollars an hour to stand there and hold a stop sign. I'll bet I could find someone to hold that stop sign for twelve dollars an hour. But the state says that's not allowed.

How insane and out of control have we truly gotten? This is not the free market that this country was founded on. If you don't believe me, look at what the unions did to the car industry. And if it had not been for President Obama bailing them out, they would have gone under. Let's look at Chrysler; while they were in bankruptcy, the bankruptcy judge gave special treatment to the unions, even though the law states that bondholders get first dibs on any money. But because of strong-arm tactics from the White House, the judge caved in and gave the union 55 percent control in the company. So now the unions own Chrysler.

If you go back and read the Fifth Amendment, you will see this is completely unlawful. It states that you can't take something without proper compensation. And the judge gave bondholders cents on the dollar. Also if you look back, some bondholders were pressured by the White House and the workers to drop their lawsuits. Now the White House denies this, but with everything that has happened since the start of President Obama's administration, I believe them. Sadly, the Supreme Court is so political these days, that they don't even follow the law or the Constitution. These people are destroying this country from the top down. The American people had better wake up and see what's happening.

Let's look at this from another angle. GM spends around sixteen hundred dollars per vehicle on health-care costs and one thousand dollars per vehicle on holiday pay, work rules, plant shutdown pay, and line relief. That's right, if a plant shuts down and the workers aren't working, GM still pays them to sit at home. How could any business stay afloat with rules like these? But on the other side, Toyota doesn't pay this. Please tell me how any company could compete against their competitors when GM is paying roughly seventy-three dollars per hour and one of their closest competitors, Toyota, is only paying around forty dollars per hour, or about half as much. But if you have your hands in the pockets of the politicians and you know they are going to bail you out, all you have to do is sit back and keep on receiving those million-dollar bonuses. And all the while the politicians keep going down the road of bankrupting our kids and grandkids. I know I keep saying it, but we the American people need to wake up before it's too late. We need to go after these corrupt politicians.

Do you realize that when the auto makers came out of bankruptcy, they actually didn't make any change or reduction in their hourly, pensions, or health-care pay? That was reported by the *Wall Street Journal* back in June 2009. They also stated, "The agreement must also be renegotiated in two years by an Obama administration running for reelection and weighing the need to keep big labor happy against the risk to taxpayer-shareholders. Who do you think wins that White House debate?" You know damn well the unions will win that debate. That's unless we the people get our butts off the couch and stand up to them. So when this happens, we need to contact our politicians to stop this.

Besides, the White House should not be involved in disputes between labor and management. You want to know how crazy it has gotten? President Obama put in the bill that the government would pay consumers a seventy-five hundred dollars tax credit to buy a GM Chevy Volt. But there is no credit for Ford. So who do you think they are going to buy an electric car from, Ford or Chevy? By the way, it is guesstimated that these new cars will cost in the range of thirty to forty thousand dollars. Even if you knock off seventy-five hundred dollars from the price of the car, the price range is still out of most people's budget. Plus, remember how the last electric car went over with the American people.

This is starting to be downright insane. We have a president who took an oath to uphold and defend the Constitution of these United States, not all the special interest groups lining his reelection coffers. Because some tree hugger or, I'm sorry, was it Al Gore who figured out a way to make a lot of money—how about over one hundred million dollars. At least the tree hugger is standing on principle, not on the backs of the American people. If Al Gore truly believed in global warning, would he be flying around in a private jet?

Now let's talk some more about the prevailing wages—in other words, union wages—against the median hourly wage for the rest of America. I am using statistics from the Bureau of Labor Statistics, and I am only using the State of California. But I'm sure it is the same way in your state, except for Texas, where their legislature only meets every two years. And Texas doesn't even have a sales tax. And get this, the legislators only get paid seven thousand dollars per year. They actually have to go back and work a real job. Boy, maybe we should put the Texas legislators in charge of Washington. I'm sure a lot more things would get done, or shall I say less.

Taken from Bureau of Labor Statistics website.

JOB DECRIPTION	UNION PAYMENTS W/ BENEFITS	MEDIAN WAGE CALIFORNIA	DIFFERENCE
	By the Hour	**By the Hour**	
FLAG MAN	**40.42/ SUNDAY 66.75**	**23.72/ SUNDAY 23.72**	16.7
TRAFFIC CONTROL	**40.42/ SUNDAY 66.75**	**23.72/ SUNDAY 23.72**	16.7

WINDOW CLEANER	**40.42/ SUNDAY 66.75**	**23.72/ SUNDAY 23.72**	16.7
FENCE BUILDER	**34.35/ SUNDAY 61.42**	**16.05/ SUNDAY 16.05**	19.30
FORKLIFT DRIVER	**45.8/ SUNDAY 73.02**	**13.95/ SUNDAY 13.95**	27.48
TRACTOR TRAILER DRIVER	**45.30/ SUNDAY 73.02**	**19.38/ SUNDAY 19.38**	25.92
CEMENT MASON	**46.84/ SUNDAY 76.34**	**23.1/ SUNDAY 23.10**	23.74
BOILER MAKER	**42.32/ SUNDAY 70.63**	**34.76/ SUNDAY 34.76**	7.56
CARPENTER	**47.22/ SUNDAY 84.57**	**24.63/ SUNDAY 24.63**	22.59

As you can see, this is insane. How can any company compete with wages like this? And every time Congress raises the minimum wage, the union wages go up again. That is why Congress is always insisting on minimum wage increases. It's not because they are looking out for the little people; it's because of the unions.

They don't care whether raising the minimum wage results in a bunch of people getting laid off, yet every time they raise it, the small business owners have to come up with those funds. That's because most small businesses work on a very tight budget. So when that budget gets squeezed, they just let one or two employees go. And, of course, that makes all the other employees have to work that much harder.

That's what's wrong with most liberals and some Republicans; they do whatever makes them feel good. But they never think about the unintended consequences. Like cash for clunkers, they first put one billion dollars into the kitty, which was supposed to last from July 2009 through November 2009. But guess what happened? When you are giving away up to forty-five hundred dollars dollars, people will show up and take it. So what does the government do when they go through one billion dollars in a week? They decide to put another couple of billions out there. But the unintended consequence is that they are destroying all the used cars the people in poverty depended on being able to buy. Another casualty was the used parts industry. So, most likely, used parts and used cars will go up in price because there will be less of them out on the street. The cash for clunkers that was started in the UK is now a permanent government program; it just might end up the same way here. Just another union giveaway by our government, and all the while we just sit back and keep taking it on the chin.

CHAPTER 6

AS CALIFORNIA GOES, SO GOES THE NATION

If you want to see what the United States will look like if we the American people don't wake up, then just look at the state of California. If we allow the Democrats to continually control the government, then just look at what they have done to the state of California in the last eight years. Of course it took more than eight years, but they have grown much bolder in the last eight years.

Under the last redistricting Democrats had control of the governor's office and both houses of the state legislature. So what they did was set up the lines so no one would get thrown out of office. And to prove this, in the last election when Republicans won over sixty seats in Congress, the Democrats swept the gambit here in California, not losing one seat.

The Democrats only go as far as we allow them. They send out little messages just to see how far we will let them. They are only interested in power, which is derived from us the people. With the help of a governor with the title of Republican in name only, they have increased the budget by almost 60 percent. We have one of the highest sales taxes in the nation, yet we are near the bottom in education. We have nearly a 50-percent dropout rate in some schools, which the Democrats love. This is due to them knowing that if they can keep us down and on the bottom, they can control us.

And we won't be able to rise to the top. Once enough of us rise to the top, they will have no choice but to turn over power. They will also no longer have the control they think they have over us. They just can't accept that we have the control over them. We are so close to bankruptcy that it is ridiculous. And all they can think to do is raise taxes.

Why is it that when people come under hard times, we must cut our budget, but when it's the government, all they can think of to do is raise our taxes? This in turn makes our hard time harder. Wouldn't it be great if, after falling on hard times, we could just go to our bosses and demand that they give us a pay raise? I'm sure the bosses wouldn't mind at all. But of course I wouldn't have any incentive to watch what I was spending.

This country used to stand on personal responsibility, on the part of not just the citizens but the politicians too. What would our founding fathers think of where we have taken this country? To think at one time the government was taking 90 percent of some Americans' money. In my view, one of the worst things this country has done is to exact income taxes on us.

We have come all the way around to the movement that started this country. This country was created to get away from the British and their high taxes. That is what the Boston Tea Party was all about. How many times do we have to look at history and see that high taxes destroy a country? Why can't people look back to the Kennedy administration when the highest tax rates were at 90 percent? And that didn't even include all the other taxes and fees that we have to pay like state, local, and utility bills (including the tax for the war of 1812, which I think is still intact). But they don't call all of them taxes; sometimes they call them usage fees. But tell me what the difference between a tax and a fee is if it's still going to the government? There is no difference; it's just a way for them to control us and to pay off their contributors.

After President Kennedy's assassination, the tax cuts he fought for were enacted. The top tax rates dropped from 90 percent to 70 percent, and the economy catapulted up. And when President Reagan dropped the rates from 70 percent to 28 percent, we got the Reagan boom, and revenue to the government almost doubled. Let's think about how less money to the government means more money to the government. A little less money can go farther if budgets are made with wisdom, but the politicians are simply spending more money than is coming in. If we have to budget our money in our households, why can't the politicians?

Why can't people see that it is the individual who creates wealth in this country, not the politician? Could someone please tell me one government program that has run efficiently? My goodness, Amtrak was taken over by the government during the Carter administration, and it has never been in the black. In other words, they have never made a profit.

Almost every single government program is in the red. and yet the Democrats are taking this country down with them. And now they want to control the health care system also. Are we out of our minds or what?—or is it our leaders who are running the loony bin? Once again, Amtrak has never made a profit since it was taken over by the federal government back in the '70s, yet we keep funding it. Where in the Constitution does it state that I'm required to provide transportation from California to DC? It doesn't; this kind of boondoggle just creates more government jobs. But we accept and go along with it because most of us either drive or fly to the places we go. But it does matter because all it does is suck more money out of the economy, and put more people on the public dole. And the more people the Democrats on the public dole, that is more people who depend on them. And I feel that this is their intention, because the more people depend on them, the more power they have over all of us.

CHAPTER 7

REAGAN THE MAN

I think there is no one who woke me up more than the man Ronald Reagan. Most politicians work every day of their lives just to get another donor. But it takes a special person to do what he did: to make life better for the American people. He wasn't interested in what was better for him, but what was better for America.

As he most famously said, "There is no limit to what a man can do or where he can go if he doesn't mind who gets the credit." That quotation demonstrates what a president should always be about. A president should be about what's best for this country, not about what's going to get him reelected or what's best for the party.

Today we have such a corrupt political system that he is most likely turning over in his grave. I don't think we have ever realized just how great he was, up until now. This man singlehandedly caused the fall of the Soviet empire without firing a single shot. This man was wise beyond his years. He realized just how powerful the word *freedom* is. He pushed aside his advisers to tell Gorbachev: "Tear down this wall!"

All I can say is please go read the Reagan letters. See how much they relate to today's times. The problem with America today is that we never go back and look at history. We only look at what we want to happen to us today, no matter what the consequences are. We brush it off and say that was just the Democrats or the Republicans. But we never look to see that the Republicans were once Democrats and the Democrats were once Republicans. Reagan once said he did not leave the Democratic Party but that the Democratic Party left him. Well, today I feel the Republican Party is leaving him and what he believed in.

Why is it so hard to make people see that the politicians are only interested in staying in power? If the country leans too far in one direction, they will follow you. And if you continue to cover your eyes and not pay attention to what they are doing, then they will just keep on leading this country in the wrong direction.

We will always have people who don't want to put forth an effort to make themselves better, and they will always try to control the system. It is up to us to keep them from destroying themselves and also this country at the same time. President Reagan was a man who always stood on principle, he always stood for something. And nearly always it was something that was good for America. Most of us are set in our ways, and we blindly follow whatever party we were brainwashed as a child to follow. And we all believe or can't accept that we can be wrong. So we put on our rose-colored glasses, block out all the negativity, and come up with some excuse as to why our party is right, even if we know deep down they are wrong. And sometimes we are all wrong, even if we can't admit it.

It's like family. You know that weird relative who always causes a problem at the family reunion? You just write it off to Uncle Jack and let it slide. But by doing this, you are only enabling that family member's bad behavior. You don't require him or her look in the mirror and say, "Maybe they're not the problem; maybe I am."

We citizens just have to have the courage to look in the mirror and ask ourselves, *What were we thinking?* I feel that we have all thought, at one time or another, that these people in Washington are truly loons. They seem to think we are too stupid to figure out what they are up to. They are wolves in sheep's clothing, and we are too wrapped up in trying to make ends meet to see what they are doing. They are leading us all to the slaughterhouse!

Good Citizenship

"Loyalty, faithfulness, commitment, courage, patriotism, the ability to distinguish between right and wrong—I hope that these values share as much a part of your life as any calculus course or social

science study. And so, do remember: gratitude is a way to a deeper wisdom. Look for that deeper wisdom. Believe me, there's great hunger for it. And here you're in luck. As Americans, you have special claim on it."

Remarks at the presentation ceremony for the
Presidential Scholars Awards
June 16, 1988

LOYALTY: Why is it that so many politicians are more loyal to the lobbyists than they are to the America people?

FAITHFULNESS: This means that you should be faithful to this country and its people. But once again, are they faithful to us and to what's best for this country? Or is it that they are only faithful to the lobbyists?

COMMITMENT: Again are our politicians committed to us the people or the lobbyists who supply all there reelection funds?

COURAGE: Tell me, do most politicians have the courage to stand up against the lobbyists and say, "I am here for the American people and not the corporations and/or the special interest groups"?

PATRIOTISM: What politician has the loyalty, faithfulness, commitment, and courage to look out for us instead of his or her own self-interest? But, no, most of them only look out for themselves and what will keep them in office. That is what made President Reagan such a great man. You always knew he was looking out for America. There was never any doubt what he cared more about; it was always this country, not himself.

I feel that President Reagan always thought of himself as a small man, but with us, the American people, behind him, he could be a great man and could accomplish almost anything. And he accomplished much more than I think even he thought he would. He took us from a glass half empty to a glass overflowing with pride.

He went from a small man to a great man, but he always kept the same shirt size.

He always had the notion that this country was just in a slump, and that we were feeling sorry for ourselves. Who hasn't gotten into feeling that way before? We were just in it on a national level. He always knew he could transform us back into the great nation that we once were. I think that until we get back to the way he made this country feel, we will not be the great country we were at that time.

President Reagan felt that he was only as good as the people who elected him. He knew he could only do as much as we the American people would allow him to do. He let us guide him on his journey to believing we could do anything, as long as we stood together. President Reagan knew that as long as we were together as a nation, we could make anything happen.

Why are we as Americans so afraid to look back on the history that he provided for us? Why are we so afraid to learn from what he did for this country? This man showed the American people what they could actually achieve. We were there, and then we forgot. We were so wrapped up in the dot-com phase of the nineties that we let our guard down. Most of us just dropped the ball and stopped paying attention to the politicians.

We may have woken up in 1994, but then we put our rose-colored glasses back on. I just hope there is another person out there with the same dreams President Reagan had. There are only two people that have made me feel the way I did when President Reagan hit the scene. The first person was a talk show host named Larry Elder who is no longer on the air. And the other person is Sarah Palin. I feel that she has sacrificed a tremendous amount because she believes in this country. And what does she get? Just a bunch of heartache from the news media. The same media who gave no scrutiny to President Obama and Vice President Joe Biden while they were running. She even went against her own Republican party in Alaska because they were corrupt.

This is one of the things we have to learn in America: if they are corrupt, no matter the person or party, challenge them, and throw them out of office. Let's just hope that people like the politicians are out there and are willing to step up to the plate, people who will give up their freedom so we can have ours. You know there have been so many men and women in the military who have given up their lives for this country, but there are also a lot of men and women who have given up their privacy. President Ronald Reagan was one of those Americans.

"This is the backbone of our country: Americans helping themselves and each other. Reaching out and finding solutions—solutions that governments and huge institutions can't find."

National Charity Awards dinner, Phoenix, Arizona, January 23, 1992

I feel that the heartbeat of America is helping each other out. Last year I donated around thirty-five hundred dollars to nonprofit organizations, but Vice President Joe Biden, according to the media, only donated around five hundred dollars.

This is where the problem lies. Democrats love to donate other people's money to the charity of their choice, whether it is welfare, Medicaid, social security, food stamps, medical care, SEC, FCC, Department of Education, Department of Homeland Security, CIA, FBI, DMV, or the thirty-two czars (so far) that President Obama has posted in his cabinet. What gives the president the right to take our money and give it to the people who helped him get elected?—which is what the czars are all about.

Tell me, after they got their posts, have you heard from them again? That is, unless there is a screwup, and the president doesn't want to answer for it, so the czar takes the fall. A czar is just a captain kickback for the people who helped Obama get elected. I think the biggest difference between liberals and conservatives is that conservatives give much more to charity than liberals do. In my opinion, conservatives believe that we the people should help take care of those who can't take care of themselves, and the liberals feel it's the government's responsibility.

I bet that if you take a dollar and put one in any charity and one in the hands of the government, the majority of the time more of the cash will go to the needy from the charity than will go from the government. This is due to all the government bureaucracies.

Poverty here in America has come to mean nothing. I don't have health care, but I do have cable TV, a stove, a new car, a cell phone. I have a CD/VHS player, plasma TV, and a computer with Internet access.

I feel that we here in America either don't know or couldn't care less how other people in the world live. There are people in Honduras who live in a shack the size of most Americans' bathrooms. How can we be so shallow to just close our eyes to how people are living in some other countries?

We here in America have the freedom to criticize the president on such trivia as how he threw a baseball at a baseball game. Rush Limbaugh spent close to a half hour on how President Obama throws like a girl. God help us if we don't get ourselves back on the right track.

The media also need to get back on track and truly look at what the government is doing. It seems that they only do that when a conservative is in power. I feel it is the media who must watch out for us the people, not to look out for the Democrats and the Republicans. I think a lot of us have fallen and gotten greedy, but I believe we can get back to what's most important, and that's family.

"We've come to a moment in our history when party labels are unimportant. Philosophy is all important. Little men with loud voices cry doom, saying little is good in America. They create fear and uncertainty among us. Millions of Americans, especially our own sons and daughters, are seeking a cause they can believe in. There is a hunger in this country today—a hunger for spiritual guidance. People yearn once again to be proud of their country and proud of themselves, and to have confidence in themselves. And there is every reason why they should be proud. Some may have failed America, but America has never failed us, and there is so much to be proud of in this land."

Remarks at the Convention of Southern GOP, Atlanta, Georgia
December 7, 1973

Boy, how can you read this and not see how it reflects today. It seems that we never learn from history in America. It seems that at times we have come full circle. It's as if we are reliving the movie *Groundhog Day*, and we will continue to do so until we truly realize what's most important in this world. And that's taking care of friends and family, standing together to really help each other out, not depending on Uncle Sam to fix every problem that comes our way. Because we all know that Uncle Sam is that drunken uncle at the family reunion. As President Reagan once said, "There is nothing more alarming than the words *I'm the government, and I'm here to help.*"

The uncle is drunk on Jack Daniels, and the government is drunk on our tax dollars. Uncle Jack can't get enough booze, and Uncle Sam can't get enough of our tax dollars. It is time for us to stand up for our country; it's time to stop blaming corporate America for all our problems. It's time to look in the mirror and say I am the master of my destiny.

Do away with the things we don't need. Isn't it strange that when I was growing up all we had was four or five channels on the TV. But today we have three or four hundred TV channels, of which we only watch four or five. When I was a child we paid nothing, and today some people pay close to one hundred dollars to watch those four or five channels. And when you add everything else you are paying for that might not be a necessity, then what right do I have to expect some other American to pay for my health care? When we all know this just gives the government more power over our lives.

We as Americans have to get our priorities straight. I think they are all screwed up. And this is all because we are told, "I am the government, and I'm here to help."

> **"In the words of Thomas Paine: "These are times that try men's souls." We need more than summer soldiers and sunshine patriots. If we believe in principles of free enterprise that made our country great, we must stand up for them again today. We must draw anew on the individual strength, ingenuity, and vision that built America. But our gaze is not set on the past; it's firmly fixed on tomorrow. We must not mortgage our children's**

future to pay for the mistakes of today. The choice before our generation is grave, but clear: we must either face and solve our problems now or surrender to them forever."

Remarks at the legislative conference of the National
Association of Realtors
March 29, 1982

We have always talked about words that have transcended time. And still we need more proof that we don't learn from our mistakes or our history. Once again we are so wrapped up in our own problems and lives that we refuse to keep up with what our politicians are doing.

Just think that in the first three months of President Obama's administration, he spent more money than all the previous presidents before him. He has taken us from around four hundred billion dollars in debt to around $1.3 trillion, all because some corporations were too big to fail.

Ask yourself: if you had no chance of running out of money because the government would bail you out, would you care about how much money you spent on your family? Of course not. That is why it is so dangerous for the government to be bailing out all these companies that only got into trouble because Fannie Mae & Freddy Mac were backed by the US government. And all these financial institutions knew they would be backed once again by a government-owned institution.

So let me get this right: the government asked financial institutions to lend to poor people, and when they said no, it was too risky, the government said that a company owned by the government would buy all these loans. What corporation would not jump on top of that deal?

I own my own company, and I would take that deal in a heartbeat. This is because we are built to take care of ourselves and do whatever is in our own best interest. That is just human nature.

We are wasting our children's money, and our grandchildren, and maybe even our great-grandchildren's, if we don't stop it right now. Our children could end up in an America that is lost. They will have an America with no promise, no ingenuity, and no drive to be the best that they can be. They will be zombies following whoever is smart enough to be leading America at that time. Let's just hope it's not Hitler.

> **"I've not taken your time this evening merely to ask you to trust me. Instead, I ask you to trust yourselves. That's what America is all about. Our struggle for nationhood, our unrelenting fight for freedom, our very existence—these have all rested on the assurance that you must be free to shape your life as you are best able to, that no one can stop you from reaching higher or take from you the creativity that has made America the envy of mankind."**

> Address to the nation on federal tax-reduction legislation,
> July 27, 1981

Can we truly understand these words? America is not great due to the government; it's because of each and every one of us. It is because of all the dreams that have come before us.

Bill Gates started a small company out of his garage and grew it into one of the largest companies in the world. Along the way, he became the richest man in the world. Ask yourself where this has happened anywhere else on the planet. And that's because all those other countries tax the hell out of their citizens.

Have you heard of an item being invented in any other country? You don't hear about it because they have no incentive. Any money they make goes straight to the government.

A guy actually took a Band-Aid and put it on his nose to open his nasal cavities and made millions helping people not to snore and to breathe easier. If the government takes all the money, then we have no incentive to better ourselves and others. I believe that the politicians don't want us to achieve our goals because that would put us in competition with them.

Think about it: someone developed a new glue and created note pads. Someone created a mobile phone even though a lot of people said he was crazy. Who is the crazy person now? That is what makes this country so great. Someone even thought of a pet rock, and he made millions. Think about that. Someone put a bunch of rocks in boxes and convinced a bunch of kids to buy them, even though they could have gone down to the nearest creek and picked one up for free. If we ever get back to the 90-percent tax rate or even close to it, we will kill initiative like that. That is truly what sets us apart from the rest of the world.

> **"Those that came to this untamed land brought family, and families built a nation. I'm convinced that today the majority of Americans want really what those first Americans wanted: a better life for themselves and their children, a minimum of government authority. Very simply, they want to be left alone in peace and safety to take care of the family by earning an honest dollar and putting away some savings. This may not sound too exciting, but there is magnificence about it. On the farm and on the street corner, in the factory and in the kitchen, millions of us ask nothing more, but certainly nothing less, than to live our own lives, according to our own values. At peace with ourselves, our neighbors, and the world."**

> National television address
> July 6, 1976

Please, God, help this country. We need to get back to those times, back when it was all about family, about doing whatever was required to take care of them.

Doesn't anyone see that when the tax rate was at 90 percent during the Kennedy era, most of what made this country great was thrown away? That is money that is sucked out of the economy. Now President Kennedy did drop the tax rate down to 70 percent. Just look at Amtrak, which has never made a profit since it was bought by the government. President Reagan dropped the rates from 70 percent to 28 percent, and what we saw was revenue doubled to the federal government. The reason was that the money was put back into the private sector where jobs were created, and those people paid taxes. The government only wastes those funds, they don't create anything. The money only gets spent on four-hundred-dollar toilet seats.

"I had a copy of the Soviet constitution and I read it with great interest. And I saw all kinds of terms in there that sound just exactly like our own: "freedom of assembly and freedom of speech" and so forth. Of course, they don't allow them to have those things, but they are in there in the constitution. But I began to wonder about the other constitutions—everyone has one—and our own, and why so much emphasis on ours. And then I found out, and the answer was very simple. That's why you don't notice it at first, but it is so great that it tells the entire difference. All those other constitutions are documents that say that "we the government allow people the following rights," and our Constitution says, "We the people allow the government the following privileges and rights." We give our permission to government to do the things that it does. And that's the whole story of the difference—why we're unique in the world and why no matter what our troubles may be, we're going to overcome all those troubles—and with your help and support because it's an ongoing process."

Remarks to delegates of the United States
Senate Youth Program
February 5, 1981

If this doesn't tell you what this country was built on and should still stand on, then I don't understand why you are still here. Can you see "we the people" or see "we the government" and still not understand which is better for our country? We the people look out for the people of this great country.

That's another problem I have with the liberals: it seems at times that all they do is bash this country. We may have had our bad times in history, but tell me, what other country has people dying to get into it? And I mean literally dying in the Mexican desert, just for a chance at getting into this great country; Asians dying in cargo containers just to get in.

All the government cares about is retaining their jobs; whichever way the polls tell them to go. Our founding fathers created a republic, not a democracy. This was because they knew that we needed it more and that sometimes like little children we can't always get everything we want. President Reagan always stood on what he believed in, not what the polls were telling him. Think back. Did you ever hear the media touting polls in the '80s? This is why I believe this country has been so successful, and why the Soviet Union collapsed. Just look at where Europe is today. Can you think of anything that has been created out of Europe in the last thirty years? That's because they are where we were in the '70s. Once again it seems no one learns from history.

"This country was founded and built by people with great dreams and the courage to take great risk."

Remarks and a question-and-answer session with members of the Massachusetts High Technology Council, Bedford, Massachusetts
January 26, 1983

Here is what the USA is truly about, what this country was founded and built on: we the people and our dreams of being what we knew we could be. And the courage to take the chance, even though we might fail. And the hopes and accolades of when we don't.

This reminds me of a quote by Marine General David M. Shoup about doers: "The galleries are full of critics. They fight no fights. They make no mistakes because they attempt nothing. Down in the arena are the doers. They make mistakes because they try many things. The man who makes no mistakes lacks boldness and the spirit of adventure. He is the brake on the wheel of progress, and yet it cannot be truly said he makes no mistakes, because his biggest mistake is the very fact that he tries nothing, does nothing, except criticize those who do things."

I think this pretty much states it all. There are the doers who aren't afraid to go out there and risk everything for the fate of their families or themselves, and then there are those who would rather depend on the government to take care of every aspect of their lives. Which one of these would you rather teach to your kids? This is why we have generational welfare and why so many of us have given up. I wrote this about life.

LIFE

It's eating us up and taking us down
There is nowhere on earth it can't be found
It's over in Africa and also in Spain
It's coming straight at us like a runaway train
But no one thinks to just step aside
All they can see is the hurt in their eyes
Why are we driven to this kind of hate?
I guess we feel it must have been fate
Why can't we just lie down and cry?
And hope to God it's all been a lie
Because you've got to give it all up
And try to build your life back up
It won't be easy, you won't feel the breeze
But believe me, someday you'll go through it with ease

In life you will always have things thrown at you that make life hard. But what you have to do is accept the situation that you are in, and then adapt to the situation the best you can, and overcome the situation by opening another door. I have always believed that when one door closes there is always another door right around the corner which opens. You just have to search for the key.

Dale Young

"Our founding fathers envisioned a nation whose strength and vitality would emerge from the ingenuity of its people and their commitment to individual liberty. They understood that a nation's prosperity is dependent on the freedom of its citizens to pursue their hopes, dreams and creative ambitions. American entrepreneurs and small business owners enthusiastically embraced the challenges of freedom, and through the miracle of the marketplace, set in motion the forces of economic growth that made our nation uniquely productive. This pattern of economic development has inspired people throughout the world to look to America for a better life."

Proclamation for Small Business Week
March 7, 1983

This is so inspiring and yet this is what this man did to this country. Does anyone truly believe that Microsoft would ever have grown like it did if President Reagan hadn't dropped the top tax rates from 70 percent to 28 percent? Would Bill Gates and Microsoft ever have happened? If the government was taking roughly 75 percent of his money when he started, do you think he would have had the ability to expand beyond his garage? In my opinion, no, but that also includes all the other people and small businesses. Why would Bill Gates or for that matter anyone have any incentive to expand their business? Taxes kill incentive and kill jobs.

Think of all the prosperity and the comforts of our lives because of Bill Gates and Microsoft. I feel President Reagan is the one who made that happen. Think of the technology we have today because of the technology boom of the late '80s and '90s. I feel that is due to President Reagan putting all that money back into the economy.

It is estimated that during President Reagan's term in office, around twenty-three million new jobs were created. In my opinion this was due to the private sector knowing what America is all about: profits. And the government never makes a profit, just look at Amtrak.

48

President Reagan was so far ahead of his generation. Will we ever see a man or woman in the future who will step up to the level President Reagan did? We are forgetting the lessons he taught us. Have we forgotten all that this man accomplished? I only pray that we never do. For you see, we never hear about people fighting to get out of the United States, only people sacrificing and fighting to get in.

"America has already succeeded where so many other historic attempts at freedom have failed. Already, we've made this cherished land the last best hope of mankind. It's up to us, in our generations, to carry on the hallowed task. It is up to us, however we may disagree on policies, to work together for progress and humanity so that our grandchildren, when they look back on us, can truly say that we not only preserved the flame of freedom, but cast its warmth and light further than those who came before us."

Remarks to the National Conference
of Christians and Jews
New York City
March 23, 1982

With this I say, Where is our flame? Is it still lit, or will we let it die out? It's as if the matches are wet, and we are hoping it doesn't rain.

What will we leave our grandchildren? What will they be taught at school? Will they even know what we once had? That's why we must stand together and do the work that's best for them and not what's best for us. We as Americans must teach them that only they can make their lives better. They are the ones who must work hard to make their lives great.

For them and their children the flame of freedom must never die! For if it does, America will die also. As President Reagan once said, "Those who have known freedom and then lost it have never known it again."

"Now you may have heard the rumors to the effect that increasing government spending is not something I'm prone to do, and to tell the truth, there's a certain substance to the rumors. At the same time, I accept without question the words of George Washington: "to be prepared for war is one of the most effectual means of preserving peace." Now, in spite of some things you may have heard, he didn't tell me that personally. Still, I'm in full agreement and believe that he did say it.

But let me seriously speak about your employers. We've been through a period in which it seemed that we the people had forgotten that the government is a convenience of, for, and by the people. And while we were busy with our own affairs, government began to grow beyond the consent of the governed. Its growth was nourished by an ever-larger share of the people's earnings that it took by taxation which became more and more confiscatory. At the same time government neglected one of its prime responsibilities—national security—as it engaged more and more in social experimentation. Our margin of safety in an increasingly hostile world was allowed to diminish, and for a time it seemed that there was an erosion of respect for the honorable profession that you have chosen."

Commencement address at the United
States Military Academy
May 27, 1981

Here is another thing that we have not learned from history. Every time we have cut our military, we have suffered the consequences. After Vietnam we slashed our military, and we got the Iran hostage crisis, we got Grenada, we got the Marine barracks in Beirut. This is because every time we cut our military, we are seen as weak by other countries.

Some countries in the outside world think just like the high school bully. Thinking we won't do anything to them, they think we are weak. After President Reagan raised funds going to the military, the Russians couldn't keep up, and their empire fell. After President Clinton cut the military, we got 9/11. But when President Bush 43 started the Afghan/Iraqi wars, we didn't hear a word from Iran. Libya even surrendered their nuclear weapons.

But as soon as we were divided in this country, Iran and North Korea started to play their games all over again. Why is it so hard for us to look back in history and learn from our mistakes? For if we don't, we will just keep making the same ones all over again. I think it is because we always have to follow the path of least resistance. We never look at the big picture; we never look back in history to see what works and what doesn't. Or perhaps we do and decide it would be too hard to stay on the right path. As the Greatest Generation found out, sometimes you have to sacrifice to get the reward.

"Freedom is the very essence of our nation. To be sure, ours is not a perfect nation. But even with our troubles, we remain the beacon of hope for oppressed peoples everywhere. Never give up the fight for freedom—a fight which, though it may never end, is the most ennobling known to man."

Presentation of a section of the Berlin Wall,
Ronald Reagan Presidential Library
April 12, 1990

This says it all: once we as Americans lose our freedom, we will be nothing. We will have given away what makes us so unique. That beacon of truth that most of us strive to reach will be gone. And if this ever happens, I truly believe, with President Reagan, that there will be no hope for mankind.

Mankind can't live without hope, for without it we have no reason to strive for excellence. We have lost the main reason to better ourselves, along with the hope that our children won't have to live in the world that we have created. For they will be slaves to the government and the people who control it. Think of it this way, people all over the world live every day with the hope that they can get to the United States so they can better themselves. With that gone, what would happen to the world?

"We who live in the free market society believe that growth, prosperity and ultimately, human fulfillment are created from the bottom up, not the government down. Only when the human spirit is allowed to invent and create, only when individuals are given a personal stake in deciding economic policies and benefiting from their success—only then can societies remain economically alive, dynamic, prosperous, progressive, and free.

Trust the people. This is one irrefutable lesson of the entire postwar period, contradicting the notion that rigid government controls are essential to economic development. The societies which have achieved the most spectacular broad-based economic progress in the shortest period of time are not the most tightly controlled, not necessarily the biggest in size or the wealthiest in natural resources. No, what united them all is their willingness to believe in the magic of the marketplace.

Everyday life confirms the fundamentally human and democratic ideal that individual effort deserves an economic reward. Nothing is more crushing to the spirit of working people and to the vision of development itself than the absence of reward for honest toil and legitimate risk. So let me speak plainly: we cannot have prosperity and successful development without economic freedom; nor can we preserve our personal and political freedom without economic freedom. Governments that set out to regiment their people with the stated objective of providing security and liberty have ended up losing both. Those which

put freedom as the first priority find they have also provided security and economic progress."

Remarks at the annual meeting of the board
of governors of the World Bank Group and
International Monetary Fund
September 29, 1981

Once again, we have proof of what this man was all about. Recall that he lowered taxes from a 70-percent rate to a 28-percent rate, and cash flow to the US government nearly doubled. When it comes to money and the cash flow, who do you think knows better how to spend it? It's the people, because they are looking to make a profit, and the government only knows how to waste it.

The government has no incentive to make a profit because it's not their money; they just end up wasting it. When was the last time during a recession that you heard of government workers being laid off? But I bet during that recession and in this one you see a lot of government jobs being created. Tell me how silly that is.

Also, when have you ever heard of a department in the government running efficiently? I have a small business, and when I ship a package, it takes UPS one day to deliver it in California. But when I ship the same package using the post office, it takes that same package up to five days to arrive. This is because the government is not out to make a profit, and UPS is.

Why is it that, when the country is in a recession, the government only thinks of raising taxes and a business only thinks of cutting the budget? That's because they have all the power, and we have none. At least that is what they have been trying to teach us to believe.

The truth is that here in America, it is we who have all the power, just as long as we stand together. Yes, all we have to do is believe and stand up for ourselves and for what's right. Why do you think they had such a hard time passing universal heath care? The Democrats had control of both houses and the presidency. It's because they heard from all of us, all those phone calls and e-mails we sent. They were scared, yet they still didn't listen. That's because they think we are weak and stupid. Let's show them just how strong we truly are by standing together.

"I'm a collector of stories that I can establish are actually told by the people of the Soviet Union among themselves. And this one has to do with the fact that in the Soviet Union, if you want to buy an automobile, there is a ten-year wait. And you have to put the money down ten years before you get the car.

So there was a young fellow there that had finally made it, and he was going through all the bureaus and agencies that he had to go through, and signing all the papers, and finally got to the last agency where they put the stamp on it. And then he gave them his money, and they said, "Come back in ten years and get your car."

And he said, "Morning or afternoon?"

And the man that had put the stamp on says, "We're talking about ten years from now. What difference does it make?"

He said, "The plumber is coming in the morning.""

Remarks at a fundraising reception for
Senator Orrin Hatch of Utah
June 17, 1987

Oh, if we here in America could only read this and truly see what national health care is going to look like in five years if not sooner. This is what a socialist country comes down to. Why is it that this country has run social security, Amtrak, Medicare, United States Postal Service, the DMV, and many more government programs into the ground? We have all heard of the six-hundred-dollar toilet seat and the three-hundred-dollar hammer. With all this evidence why would we trust the government with a program that big?

We are told that on the average corporations spend fifteen thousand dollars per person on health care. But when universal health care kicks in, the penalty for not covering your employees is only eight thousand dollars. So why wouldn't a smart businessperson just force employees to go on the government program? The purpose of being in business is to make a profit.

But you know what? The politicians did this on purpose. They want as many people as possible on the government plan because it gives them that much more power over us. And when business does this, the politicians will just say, "I told you so, those mean old executives only care about money and not you." And we will just go along like sheep to the slaughterhouse.

No one really cares that it was the government who actually caused the health-care crisis. It all started back during the FDR administration when he put wage restrictions on businesses during the Great Depression. So for businesses to keep the best and brightest, they came up with health care.

Once again here is a good lesson: whenever the government comes up with a law that hurts business or the little guy, they always figure a way around it. That's why no matter how hard the politicians think they are helping us, they just end up hurting us, at least the majority of us. Once health care was taken over by business and taken out of the people's hands, we no longer cared what it cost because someone else was paying for it. If someone was paying for the gas in your car, would you care if it was at four or five dollars a gallon? And that is exactly the problem with health care; we took it out of the people's hands.

On top of that, we are not allowed to shop in other states for health care. Some states only have two insurance companies to pick from. And there are around thirteen hundred insurance companies doing business in this country. Competition is what will bring down the cost, if they will just let everybody shop across state lines.

We are going back to the days when the coal mine is paying you to work, but they also own the company store where you buy everything and also the house you are renting. This is what you call the classic double cross. I have another name for it: slavery.

"Let it never be said of this generation of Americans that we became so obsessed with failure that we refused to take risks that could further the cause of peace and freedom in the world."

State of the Union Address
January 27, 1987

These words speak loudly because we as Americans are so obsessed with our own lives that we could not care less what is happening to this country. No one is willing to risk anything to make this country what it once was.

We see so much happening in the rest of the world. Think of all those countries where people are oppressed. If we go out and help those people get what we have in this country, at least for now we might have to sacrifice. We may have to give a little; we may have to sacrifice that four-dollar latte. How can we be so selfish here in America? How can we be so greedy?

We were once a great nation that freed Europe from a madman. We are at that same place in time. At first we said it's not our problem; let them sort it out for themselves. But we eventually came to the conclusion that as goes Europe so goes the United States. If we had allowed this man to accomplish what he had set out to do, he would have set his eyes on his next goal. And most likely it would have been on us. That was the Greatest Generation who sacrificed so much for this country.

But I am afraid that too many of them have left us. Are we as strong as they were? They are the ones who gave all to save this country and the world. Will we forget them? Will we fail those young men and women now fighting overseas to protect this country? We can't let their sacrifices of years past be forgotten. God help us if we do, for I feel He will give up on us.

"Our government has no power except that granted it by the people. It is time to check and reverse the growth of government, which shows signs of having grown beyond the consent of the governed. It is my intention to curb the size and influence of the federal establishment and to demand recognition of the distinction between the powers granted to the federal government and those reserved to the states or to the people. All of us need to be reminded that the federal government did not create the states; the states created the federal government."

Inaugural Address
January 20, 1981

Why can't we the American people figure out that the federal government has no power that isn't granted by the people? And there is the problem: we the people have spoiled our politicians as if they were our children. Not paying attention, we have let them get away with too much.

How many of us are truly paying attention to what's going on in America? When Congress is sworn into office, they all swear to uphold the Constitution, but all they do is shred it. Where in the Constitution does it state that the federal government is to supply all Americans with health care? This country has survived for over two hundred years without it. It wasn't until the government got involved that it got out of control.

Once again, it was during the Great Depression that the government put controls on how much a company could pay its employees—also not in the Constitution. Businesses that were losing their best employees had to come up with a solution to keep them or draw some from other companies' people and the solution happened to be health care. Just think about it, if the government paid your auto bills, would you really care about getting that oil change?

I have seen what free health care becomes while serving in the Marine Corps. If you had to go to the emergency room, it was a four- to six-hour wait. If you got a cold, you would just go down and get some cough syrup. Why not, if you don't have to pay for it? And when the government's programs fully kick in, what incentive will your employer have to give it to you? They will just let you go on the government's dime to help their bottom line.

The Democrats know this is going to happen, and they're just going to bide their time. Why do you think they were vague and didn't give us the details? Because they learned their lesson with Hillary care.

"In eight short years, we have reversed a fifty-year trend of turning to the government for solutions. We have learned creativity that makes a great nation. Just as the first American Revolution, which began with the shot heard round the world, inspired people everywhere who dreamed of freedom, so has this second American Revolution inspired

changes throughout the world. The message that we brought to Washington—reduce government, reduce regulation, restore incentives—has been heard around the world. I leave this office secure in the knowledge that these policies have worked, and confident that this great nation will continue to lead the way toward freedom and prosperity for all mankind."

Letter accompanying the president's
annual economic report
January 10, 1989

You have to go back to that day and time to truly realize what President Reagan did for this country. What other president has taken this country from despair to hope in so little time? He made us believe once again in this country and ourselves.

All you hear today from President Obama and his cohorts is how bad this country is, even going overseas and apologizing for America. We are the greatest nation on this earth. We have more with which to help many countries than any other nation.

Was President Reagan a once-in-a-lifetime phenomenon? I feel God knew what we were doing to ourselves, and He sent President Reagan to us to pick this country back up and give us something to believe in—ourselves. When President Reagan came into office, this country was in so much disrepair, he was the right man at the right time.

I feel President Reagan sacrificed a great deal for this country, even lying on a surgical table after the assassination attempt. This man had the courage and humor to tell the surgeon, "I hope you're a Republicans," to which the surgeon replied, "Today we are all Republican, Mr. President." Please ask yourself, if you were on your deathbed, would this be your response?

This man tried everything he could to shrink the government. But he knew he had to work with the Democrats. So he would get together with Tip O'Neill, the Speaker of the House at that time. He worked hand in hand with him to work out their differences. President Reagan never let his pride get in the way; in fact, he once stated that "there is no limit to what a man can do or where he can go if he doesn't mind who gets the credit."

I think President Reagan treated us as his own children, and he would do anything he could to make all our lives better. He sacrificed then so our lives would be better off now. But today we are letting his dream slip away. We are spoiled children wasting away our inheritance, not seeing what tomorrow will bring.

CHAPTER 8

CAP AND TRADE

Here we go again, believing what the politicians want us to believe. "Global warming is destroying the planet," when all we have to do is follow the money. If cap and trade is passed, where do you think all the money will go? Or where will it come from? Of course it will come from all of us, the American people.

If corporate America gets taxed, where do you think they will get the money to cover the cost? They will get it from us by raising the prices on the goods we buy, which in turn means inflation, which we all know means an indirect tax from the government. But the government doesn't get the blame; instead, it is the evil corporation. This is also the evil corporation that hired you and is helping take care of you and your family. If they didn't raise the prices on their products, they would have to let you go.

Tell me which helps better you and your family's life. Is it the person who hired you to do a job or the government which does nothing for you? With a corporation you have an incentive to better your life if you work hard. But with the government you have an incentive to just sit at home and watch *Jerry Springer*. This is their way of blaming the evil corporation for the way America is so screwed up. And the bonus is they don't get blamed for raising taxes.

The politicians just love to raise fees on everything. Then they go out to those same evil corporations and ask for money to be donated to their political action committees, in return for which they will put a little loophole in another bill. And the politician gets reelected, and the corporation is exempted from paying the fee.

But the small businesses don't have the money to drive this gravy train. So to survive they have to raise prices. I own a small business, and I will do anything it takes to survive and protect my family. It is the corrupt politicians who don't do anything but extort what they need to stay in office. And this is what corrupts the system.

If we didn't have all this corruption in Washington and all the state houses, then there would be no need for lobbyists in every capital in the nation. And when the politicians get fired by the people, they just go and get a job with those same lobbyists. Congress should go back to being a part-time job; this would give them less control over the American people and the states.

President Obama himself stated that electric bills would skyrocket if cap and trade was passed. And when those bills skyrocket, the price of everything will go up. This is because business will pass all those costs down to the consumer. All you have to do is follow the money. No matter what you are looking into in Washington, all you have to do is follow the money trail.

It is human nature to want what's best for your family. Would you rather have your family living in South Central Los Angeles or in Beverly Hills? But the politicians have taken this mantra too far. The way they are doing it is hurting the American people. What is wrong is the politicians think they know what's best for you and me. How can a politician in New York know what's best for you in Texas, and vice versa? It's time for the states to take back the power that the US government has taken from them. The federal government should go back to only doing what the Constitution says it is allowed to do.

Vice President Al Gore started a company that will directly profit from the cap and trade bill. Do you truly feel that he is doing all of this for the environment? Can we all just use some common sense when talking about climate change? This is all about raising money for personal gain. Vice President Al Gore has grown his own portfolio by over one hundred million dollars since he started this campaign.

As we have said before, just follow the money. This is all about raising taxes so they can fund the next earmark that goes to the person who funded their last campaign. They only care about staying in power—while they keep us from looking in their left hand because their next project is sitting in their right. And we are so focused on the left that we ignore the right.

CHAPTER 9

PORK-BARREL SPENDING

A Sample of the 9,287 Omnibus Bill Earmarks

Amount	Recipient/Purpose	Congressional Sponsor
$1,049,000	Mormon Crickets, Utah	Bennett
$475,000	Sidewalk Construction in Ashland & Cherryland, CA	Lee
$225,000	Everybody Wins!	LaHood
$200,000	Tattoo removal program in Mission Hills, CA	Berman
$190,000	Buffalo Bill Historical Center, Cody, WY	Cubin
$237,500	Theater renovation, Merced, CA	Cardoza
$75,000	Totally Teen Zone, Albany, GA	Bishop, Chambliss

$500,000	National History Day	several lawmakers
$570,000	Ronald Reagan Parkway, Boone County, IN	Buyer
$100,000	Gulf of Maine Lobster Foundation	Allen, Snowe, Collins
$332,500	Build a school sidewalk, Franklin, TX	Edwards (TX)
$381,000	George Eastman House, Rochester, NY	Slaughter, Schumer
$380,600	Versailles Borough Stray Gas Mitigation	Doyle (PA)
$75,000	Wayne Gomes Youth Baseball Diversity Foundation	Scott
$381,000	Jazz at Lincoln Center, New York, NY	Nadler
$5,813,000	Edward M. Kennedy Institute for the Senate, Boston, MA	Kerry, Byrd, Harkin, Durbin, Mikulski, Dodd
$950,000	Bus and Bus Facilities, Lawrence, KS	Moore, Roberts
$300,000	Montana World Trade Center	Rehberg
$2,673,000	Wood Education and Resource Center	President, Byrd

$380,000	Lemon Street Reconstruction and Enhancements, FL	Bilirakis
$17,500,000	FDR Presidential Library renovation	Gillibrand, Reid, Schumer
$2,000,000	LBJ Presidential Library	Hutchison
$22,000,000	JFK Presidential Library	Markey, Lynch, Kerry
$300,000	GoGirlGo! Boston, MA	Capuano, Kennedy, Kerry
$285,000	Kansas Farm Bureau, Manhattan, KS	Brownback
$6,838,000	John F. Kennedy Center for the Performing Arts	several lawmakers
$427,500	Bicycle/Pedestrian Pathways, Provo, UT	Cannon, Hatch
$950,000	World Trade Center of St. Louis, MO	Bond
$725,000	Illinois Height Modernization	Johnson (IL), LaHood
$298,257	Small business program, Florida Department of Citrus	Boyd, Putnam, Martinez
$237,500	Sidewalk Construction, Vienna, VA	Davis (VA)

$190,000	Bishop Museum, Honolulu, HI	Inouye
$100,000	Police Athletic League of Buffalo, Inc	Slaughter
$206,000	Wool Research	Conaway, Rodriguez (TX)
$475,000	5th & Market St. Transportation Improvements, PA	Specter
$494,000	Business incubator, Arkansas State University	Berry, Lincoln, Pryor
$400,000	Salisbury House, Des Moines, IA	Harkin, Grassley, Boswell
$138,000	John Nance Garner Museum, Austin, TX	Rodriguez (TX)
$190,000	Sidewalk Improvements, Williamstown, VT	Leahy, Sanders
$870,000	Red Wolf Breeding Facility Relocation	Shuler
$190,000	George C. Wallace Community College-Dothan, AL	Everett
$142,500	Pregones Theater, Bronx, NY	Serrano

$6,623,000	Formosan Subterranean Termites Research	Landrieu, Vitter, Alexander
$1,903,000	Landfill Gas Utilization Plant in NY	Schumer
$475,000	Replacement of Bus Fleet, Topeka, KS	Boyda
$285,000	Widening of County Road 222, Cullman, AL	Aderholt
$2,192,000	Center for Grape Genetics, Geneva, NY	Schumer, Walsh, Hinchey, Arcuri
$1,791,000	Swine Odor and Manure Management Research, Ames, IA	Harkin
$950,000	Bossier Parish Congestion Relief Plan, LA	Landrieu, Vitter
$712,500	Replacement Buses, Detroit, MI	Conyers, Levin, Stabenow
$4,545,000	Wood Utilization Research	several lawmakers
$200,000	Oil Region Alliance	Peterson (PA)
$2,565,000	Renovate the Cox Building, Maysville, KY	McConnell, Davis (KY)
$400,000	Minnesota Teen Challenge	Ramstad, Coleman
$190,000	Berkshire Theater Festival, Stockbridge, MA	Kennedy, Kerry

$4,750,000	Shiloh Road, MT	Baucus, Tester
$143,000	American Ballet Theatre, New York, NY	Maloney, Schumer
$100,000	Ready, Willing & Able, Philadelphia,	Brady (PA)
$250,000	Lederer Theater, Providence, RI	Reed
$1,187,500	Wolf Trap Performing Arts Multi-Use Trail, Fairfax, VA	Moran
$3,800,000	Old Tiger Stadium Conservancy, MI	Levin
$294,500	Jackie Joyner-Kersee Center, East St. Louis, IL	Durbin
$143,000	Historic Jazz Foundation, Inc., Kansas City, MO	Cleaver, Emanuel
$1,000,000	Cal Ripken Sr. Foundation	Ruppersberger, Mikulski, Shelby
$237,500	Street Rehabilitation, Doral, FL	Diaz-Balart (Lincoln)
$49,134	Bronx Council on the Arts	Serrano
$475,000	Pedestrian Bridges, Iowa City, IA	Loebsack

$167,000	Autry National Center for the American West, Los Angeles, CA	Schiff, McKeon, Bono, Boxer
$315,000	Music education, Carnegie Hall, New York, NY	Maloney, Schumer
$122,821	Greater Toledo Arts Commission	Kaptur
$950,000	55th Street East Grade Separation, Minot, ND	Dorgan, Conrad
$951,500	Energy Efficiency Street Lighting, Detroit, MI	Kilpatrick, Levin, Stabenow
$143,000	Stockbridge-Munsee Museum, Bowler, WI	Kagen
$475,000	Italian American Museum, New York, NY	Ackerman, Nadler
$1,217,000	Citrus Canker, Greening, FL	several lawmakers
$900,000	Adler Planetarium and Astronomy Museum, Chicago, IL	Jackson Jr., Emanuel, Davis (IL)
$142,500	Bus Replacement, Culver City, CA	Watson
$2,150,000	Wisconsin Height Modernization	Obey
$1,900,000	Hattiesburg 4th Street Improvements, MS	Cochran, Wicker

$71,000	Dance Theater Etcetera, Brooklyn, NY	Velázquez
$333,000	Museum of Aviation, Warner Robins, GA	Marshall (GA), Isakson
$1,235,000	Reconstruction and Upgrade 2300 West Street, Lehi, UT	Hatch, Cannon
$380,000	Revitalize Aliceville, AL	Shelby
$150,000	Nashua Police Athletic League Youth Safe Haven	Hodes, Gregg
$237,500	Paving, sidewalks and streetlights, Islip, NY	Israel
$238,000	Museum of Fine Arts, Boston, MA	Kennedy, Kerry
$1,425,000	I-85 Widening, NC	Burr, Dole, Hayes, Watt
$285,000	Sun Valley Lighting Project, CA	Berman
$119,000	Children's Discovery Museum, San Jose, CA	Honda, Lofgren
$385,000	World Trade Center, Utah	Bishop (UT), Bennett
$300,000	Shakespeare and Company	Oliver, Kennedy, Kerry

$476,000	National Council of La Raza in Washington DC	Menendez, Bingaman
$508,000	Karnal Bunt, Manhattan, KS	Brownback, Roberts, Moran, Boyda, Tiahrt
$300,000	Fairplex Trade and Conference Center	Dreier, Napolitano
$237,500	SR-91 Congestion Relief, Orange County, CA	Miller (CA)
$380,000	Construction of On/Off Ramps, Midland, TX	Conaway
$380,600	Carbon Neutral Green Campus, NV	Porter, Reid
$150,000	Manufacturers Association of Central New York	Walsh
$475,000	Calhoun County Highway 1 Resurfacing, IL	Hare
$45,000	Weed It Now on the Berkshire, MA	Olver
$24,000	A+For Abstinence, Waynesboro, PA	Specter
$819,000	Catfish Genome, Auburn, AL	Shelby, Rogers (AL), Everett, Davis (AL)
$196,514	Beaver Street Enterprise Center, Jacksonville, FL	Brown (FL), Martinez

$75,000	Chattahoochee County Family Connection	Bishop
$2,188,450	Bismarck State College Center Of Excellence Laboratories, ND	Dorgan
$469,000	Fruit fly facility, HI	Akaka, Inouye, Hirono
$800,000	Oyster rehabilitation, AL	Shelby
$238,000	Ed Roberts Campus, Berkeley, CA	Boxer
$475,000	55th Street Extension, Rochester, MN	Donnelly, Lugar

Source: Conference Report of HR 1105

I have but a few things to say about this chapter because it says enough on its own. Why not have a constitutional amendment that states that no money will be spent by the federal government, unless it benefits everyone in America. If you want to find money for tattoo removal, then you should be able to raise it locally. Why should someone in Texas have to pay for a bridge to nowhere in Alaska? Alaska should be able to raise the funds on its own.

CHAPTER 10

US CONSTITUTION

We the People of the United States, in Order to form a more perfect Union, Establish Justice, insure domestic Tranquility, provide for the common defense, promote the general Welfare, and secure the Blessings of Liberty to ourselves and our Posterity, do ordain and establish this Constitution for the United States of America.

Article 1.

Section 1
All legislative Powers herein granted shall be vested in a Congress of the United States, which shall consist of a Senate and House of Representatives.

Section 2
The House of Representatives shall be composed of Members chosen every second Year by the People of the several States, and the Electors in each State shall have the Qualifications requisite for Electors of the most numerous Branch of the State Legislature.

No Person shall be a Representative who shall not have attained to the Age of twenty five Years, and been seven Years a Citizen of the United States, and who shall not, when elected, be an Inhabitant of that State in which he shall be chosen.

Representatives and direct Taxes shall be apportioned among the several States which may be included within this Union, according to their respective Numbers, which shall be determined by adding to the whole Number of free Persons, including those bound to Service for a Term of Years, and excluding Indians not taxed, three fifths of all other Persons.

The actual Enumeration shall be made within three Years after the first Meeting of the Congress of the United States, and within every subsequent Term of ten Years, in such Manner as they shall by Law direct. The Number of Representatives shall not exceed one for every thirty Thousand, but each State shall have at Least one Representative; and until such enumeration shall be made, the State of New Hampshire shall be entitled to choose three, Massachusetts eight, Rhode Island and Providence Plantations one, Connecticut five, New York six, New Jersey four, Pennsylvania eight, Delaware one, Maryland six, Virginia ten, North Carolina five, South Carolina five and Georgia three.

When vacancies happen in the Representation from any State, the Executive Authority thereof shall issue Writs of Election to fill such Vacancies.

The House of Representatives shall choose their Speaker and other Officers; and shall have the sole Power of Impeachment.

Section 3
The Senate of the United States shall be composed of two Senators from each State, chosen by the Legislature thereof, for six Years; and each Senator shall have one Vote.

Immediately after they shall be assembled in Consequence of the first Election, they shall be divided as equally as may be into three Classes. The Seats of the Senators of the first Class shall be vacated at the Expiration of the second Year, of the second Class at the Expiration of the fourth Year, and of the third Class at the Expiration of the sixth Year, so that one third may be chosen every second Year; and if Vacancies happen by Resignation, or otherwise, during the Recess of the Legislature of any State, the Executive thereof may make temporary Appointments until the next Meeting of the Legislature, which shall then fill such Vacancies.

No person shall be a Senator who shall not have attained to the Age of thirty Years, and been nine Years a Citizen of the United States, and who shall not, when elected, be an Inhabitant of that State for which he shall be chosen.

The Vice President of the United States shall be President of the Senate, but shall have no Vote, unless they be equally divided.

The Senate shall choose their other Officers, and also a President pro tempore, in the absence of the Vice President, or when he shall exercise the Office of President of the United States.

The Senate shall have the sole Power to try all Impeachments. When sitting for that Purpose, they shall be on Oath or Affirmation. When the President of the United States is tried, the Chief Justice shall preside: And no Person shall be convicted without the Concurrence of two thirds of the Members present.

Judgment in Cases of Impeachment shall not extend further than to removal from Office, and disqualification to hold and enjoy any Office of honor, Trust or Profit under the United States: but the Party convicted shall nevertheless be liable and subject to Indictment, Trial, Judgment and Punishment, according to Law.

Section 4
The Times, Places and Manner of holding Elections for Senators and Representatives, shall be prescribed in each State by the Legislature thereof; but the Congress may at any time by Law make or alter such Regulations, except as to the Place of Choosing Senators.

The Congress shall assemble at least once in every Year, and such Meeting shall be on the first Monday in December, unless they shall by Law appoint a different Day.

Section 5

Each House shall be the Judge of the Elections, Returns and Qualifications of its own Members, and a Majority of each shall constitute a Quorum to do Business; but a smaller number may adjourn from day to day, and may be authorized to compel the Attendance of absent Members, in such Manner, and under such Penalties as each House may provide.

Each House may determine the Rules of its Proceedings, punish its Members for disorderly Behavior, and, with the Concurrence of two-thirds, expel a Member.

Each House shall keep a Journal of its Proceedings, and from time to time publish the same, excepting such Parts as may in their Judgment require Secrecy; and the Yeas and Nays of the Members of either House on any question shall, at the Desire of one fifth of those Present, be entered on the Journal.

Neither House, during the Session of Congress, shall, without the Consent of the other, adjourn for more than three days, nor to any other Place than that in which the two Houses shall be sitting.

Section 6

The Senators and Representatives shall receive a Compensation for their Services, to be ascertained by Law, and paid out of the Treasury of the United States. They shall in all Cases, except Treason, Felony and Breach of the Peace, be privileged from Arrest during their Attendance at the Session of their respective Houses, and in going to and returning from the same; and for any Speech or Debate in either House, they shall not be questioned in any other Place.

No Senator or Representative shall, during the Time for which he was elected, be appointed to any civil Office under the Authority of the United States which shall have been created, or the Emoluments whereof shall have been increased during such time; and no Person holding any Office under the United States, shall be a Member of either House during his Continuance in Office.

Section 7

All bills for raising Revenue shall originate in the House of Representatives; but the Senate may propose or concur with Amendments as on other Bills.

Every Bill which shall have passed the House of Representatives and the Senate, shall, before it become a Law, be presented to the President of the United States; If he approve he shall sign it, but if not he shall return it, with his Objections to that House in which it shall have originated, who shall enter the Objections at large on their Journal, and proceed to reconsider it. If after such Reconsideration two thirds of that House shall agree to pass the Bill, it shall be sent, together with the Objections, to the other House, by which it shall likewise be reconsidered, and if approved by two thirds of that House, it shall become a Law. But in all such Cases the Votes of both Houses shall be determined by Yeas and Nays, and the Names of the Persons voting for and against the Bill shall be entered on the Journal of each House respectively. If any Bill shall not be returned by the President within ten Days (Sundays excepted) after it shall have been presented to him, the Same shall be a Law, in like Manner as if he had signed it, unless the Congress by their Adjournment prevent its Return, in which Case it shall not be a Law.

Every Order, Resolution, or Vote to which the Concurrence of the Senate and House of Representatives may be necessary (except on a question of Adjournment) shall be presented to the President of the United States; and before the Same shall take Effect, shall be approved by him, or being disapproved by him, shall be repassed by two thirds of the Senate and House of Representatives, according to the Rules and Limitations prescribed in the Case of a Bill.

Section 8
The Congress shall have Power To lay and collect Taxes, Duties, Imposts and Excises, to pay the Debts and provide for the common Defence and general Welfare of the United States; but all Duties, Imposts and Excises shall be uniform throughout the United States;

To borrow money on the credit of the United States;

To regulate Commerce with foreign Nations, and among the several States, and with the Indian Tribes;

To establish an uniform Rule of Naturalization, and uniform Laws on the subject of Bankruptcies throughout the United States;

To coin Money, regulate the Value thereof, and of foreign Coin, and fix the Standard of Weights and Measures;

To provide for the Punishment of counterfeiting the Securities and current Coin of the United States;

To establish Post Offices and Post Roads;

To promote the Progress of Science and useful Arts, by securing for limited Times to Authors and Inventors the exclusive Right to their respective Writings and Discoveries;

To constitute Tribunals inferior to the supreme Court;

To define and punish Piracies and Felonies committed on the high Seas, and Offenses against the Law of Nations;

To declare War, grant Letters of Marque and Reprisal, and make Rules concerning Captures on Land and Water;

To raise and support Armies, but no Appropriation of Money to that Use shall be for a longer Term than two Years;

To provide and maintain a Navy;

To make Rules for the Government and Regulation of the land and naval Forces;

To provide for calling forth the Militia to execute the Laws of the Union, suppress Insurrections and repel Invasions;

To provide for organizing, arming, and disciplining the Militia, and for governing such Part of them as may be employed in the Service of the United States, reserving to the States respectively, the Appointment of the Officers, and the Authority of training the Militia according to the discipline prescribed by Congress;

To exercise exclusive Legislation in all Cases whatsoever, over such District (not exceeding ten Miles square) as may, by Cession of particular States, and the acceptance of Congress, become the Seat of the Government of the United States, and to exercise like Authority over all Places purchased by the Consent of the Legislature of the State in which the Same shall be, for the Erection of Forts, Magazines, Arsenals, dock-Yards, and other needful Buildings; And

To make all Laws which shall be necessary and proper for carrying into Execution the foregoing Powers, and all other Powers vested by this Constitution in the Government of the United States, or in any Department or Officer thereof.

Section 9
The Migration or Importation of such Persons as any of the States now existing shall think proper to admit, shall not be prohibited by the Congress prior to the Year one thousand eight hundred and eight, but a tax or duty may be imposed on such Importation, not exceeding ten dollars for each Person.

The privilege of the Writ of Habeas Corpus shall not be suspended, unless when in Cases of Rebellion or Invasion the public Safety may require it.

No Bill of Attainder or ex post facto Law shall be passed.

No capitation, or other direct, Tax shall be laid, unless in Proportion to the Census or Enumeration herein before directed to be taken.

No Tax or Duty shall be laid on Articles exported from any State.

No Preference shall be given by any Regulation of Commerce or Revenue to the Ports of one State over those of another: nor shall Vessels bound to, or from, one State, be obliged to enter, clear, or pay Duties in another.

No Money shall be drawn from the Treasury, but in Consequence of Appropriations made by Law; and a regular Statement and Account of the Receipts and Expenditures of all public Money shall be published from time to time.

No Title of Nobility shall be granted by the United States: And no Person holding any Office of Profit or Trust under them, shall, without the Consent of the Congress, accept of any present, Emolument, Office, or Title, of any kind whatever, from any King, Prince or foreign State.

Section 10
No State shall enter into any Treaty, Alliance, or Confederation; grant Letters of Marque and Reprisal; coin Money; emit Bills of Credit; make any Thing but gold and silver Coin a Tender in Payment of Debts; pass any Bill of Attainder, ex post facto Law, or Law impairing the Obligation of Contracts, or grant any Title of Nobility.

No State shall, without the Consent of the Congress, lay any Imposts or Duties on Imports or Exports, except what may be absolutely necessary for executing its inspection Laws: and the net Produce of all Duties and Imposts, laid by any State on Imports or Exports, shall be for the Use of the Treasury of the United States; and all such Laws shall be subject to the Revision and Control of the Congress.

No State shall, without the Consent of Congress, lay any duty of Tonnage, keep Troops, or Ships of War in time of Peace, enter into any Agreement or Compact with another State, or with a foreign Power, or engage in War, unless actually invaded, or in such imminent Danger as will not admit of delay.

Article 2.

Section 1
The executive Power shall be vested in a President of the United States of America. He shall hold his Office during the Term of four Years, and, together with the Vice-President chosen for the same Term, be elected, as follows:

Each State shall appoint, in such Manner as the Legislature thereof may direct, a Number of Electors, equal to the whole Number of Senators and Representatives to which the State may be entitled in the Congress: but no Senator or Representative, or Person holding an Office of Trust or Profit under the United States, shall be appointed an Elector.

The Electors shall meet in their respective States, and vote by Ballot for two persons, of whom one at least shall not lie an Inhabitant of the same State with themselves. And they shall make a List of all the Persons voted for, and of the Number of Votes for each; which List they shall sign and certify, and transmit sealed to the Seat of the Government of the United States, directed to the President of the Senate. The President of the Senate shall, in the Presence of the Senate and House of Representatives, open all the Certificates, and the Votes shall then be counted. The Person having the greatest Number of Votes shall be the President, if such Number be a Majority of the whole Number of Electors appointed; and if there be more than one who have such Majority, and have an equal Number of Votes, then the House of Representatives shall immediately choose by Ballot one of them for President; and if no Person have a Majority, then from the five highest on the List the said House shall in like Manner choose the President. But in choosing the President, the Votes shall be taken by States, the Representation from each State having one Vote; a quorum for this Purpose shall consist of a Member or Members from two-thirds of the States, and a Majority of all the States shall be necessary to a Choice. In every Case, after the Choice of the President, the Person having the greatest Number of Votes of the Electors shall be the Vice President. But if there should remain two or more who have equal Votes, the Senate shall choose from them by Ballot the Vice-President.

The Congress may determine the Time of choosing the Electors, and the Day on which they shall give their Votes; which Day shall be the same throughout the United States.

No person except a natural born Citizen, or a Citizen of the United States, at the time of the Adoption of this Constitution, shall be eligible to the Office of President; neither shall any Person be eligible to that Office who shall not have attained to the Age of thirty-five Years, and been fourteen Years a Resident within the United States.

In Case of the Removal of the President from Office, or of his Death, Resignation, or Inability to discharge the Powers and Duties of the said Office, the same shall devolve on the Vice President, and the Congress may by Law provide for the Case of Removal, Death, Resignation or Inability, both of the President and Vice President, declaring what Officer shall then act as President, and such Officer shall act accordingly, until the Disability be removed, or a President shall be elected.

The President shall, at stated Times, receive for his Services, a Compensation, which shall neither be increased nor diminished during the Period for which he shall have been elected, and he shall not receive within that Period any other Emolument from the United States, or any of them.

Before he enter on the Execution of his Office, he shall take the following Oath or Affirmation:

"I do solemnly swear (or affirm) that I will faithfully execute the Office of President of the United States, and will to the best of my Ability, preserve, protect and defend the Constitution of the United States."

Section 2

The President shall be Commander in Chief of the Army and Navy of the United States, and of the Militia of the several States, when called into the actual Service of the United States; he may require the Opinion, in writing, of the principal Officer in each of the executive Departments, upon any subject relating to the Duties of their respective Offices, and he shall have Power to Grant Reprieves and Pardons for Offenses against the United States, except in Cases of Impeachment.

He shall have Power, by and with the Advice and Consent of the Senate, to make Treaties, provided two thirds of the Senators present concur; and he shall nominate, and by and with the Advice and Consent of the Senate, shall appoint Ambassadors, other public Ministers and Consuls, Judges of the supreme Court, and all other Officers of the United States, whose Appointments are not herein otherwise provided for, and which shall be established by Law: but the Congress may by Law vest the Appointment of such inferior Officers, as they think proper, in the President alone, in the Courts of Law, or in the Heads of Departments.

The President shall have Power to fill up all Vacancies that may happen during the Recess of the Senate, by granting Commissions which shall expire at the End of their next Session.

Section 3

He shall from time to time give to the Congress Information of the State of the Union, and recommend to their Consideration such Measures as he shall judge necessary and expedient; he may, on extraordinary Occasions, convene both Houses, or either of them, and in Case of Disagreement between them, with Respect to the Time of Adjournment, he may adjourn them to such Time as he shall think proper; he shall receive Ambassadors and other public Ministers; he shall take Care that the Laws be faithfully executed, and shall Commission all the Officers of the United States.

Section 4
The President, Vice President and all civil Officers of the United States, shall be removed from Office on Impeachment for, and Conviction of, Treason, Bribery, or other high Crimes and Misdemeanors.

Article 3.

Section 1
The judicial Power of the United States, shall be vested in one supreme Court, and in such inferior Courts as the Congress may from time to time ordain and establish. The Judges, both of the supreme and inferior Courts, shall hold their Offices during good Behavior, and shall, at stated Times, receive for their Services a Compensation which shall not be diminished during their Continuance in Office.

Section 2
The judicial Power shall extend to all Cases, in Law and Equity, arising under this Constitution, the Laws of the United States, and Treaties made, or which shall be made, under their Authority; to all Cases affecting Ambassadors, other public Ministers and Consuls; to all Cases of admiralty and maritime Jurisdiction; to Controversies to which the United States shall be a Party; to Controversies between two or more States; between a State and Citizens of another State; between Citizens of different States; between Citizens of the same State claiming Lands under Grants of different States, and between a State, or the Citizens thereof, and foreign States, Citizens or Subjects.

In all Cases affecting Ambassadors, other public Ministers and Consuls, and those in which a State shall be Party, the supreme Court shall have original Jurisdiction. In all the other Cases before mentioned, the supreme Court shall have appellate Jurisdiction, both as to Law and Fact, with such Exceptions, and under such Regulations as the Congress shall make.

The Trial of all Crimes, except in Cases of Impeachment, shall be by Jury; and such Trial shall be held in the State where the said

Crimes shall have been committed; but when not committed within any State, the Trial shall be at such Place or Places as the Congress may by Law have directed.

Section 3
Treason against the United States, shall consist only in levying War against them, or in adhering to their Enemies, giving them Aid and Comfort. No Person shall be convicted of Treason unless on the Testimony of two Witnesses to the same overt Act, or on Confession in open Court.

The Congress shall have power to declare the Punishment of Treason, but no Attainder of Treason shall work Corruption of Blood, or Forfeiture except during the Life of the Person attainted.

Article 4.

Section 1
Full Faith and Credit shall be given in each State to the public Acts, Records, and judicial Proceedings of every other State. And the Congress may by general Laws prescribe the Manner in which such Acts, Records and Proceedings shall be proved, and the Effect thereof.

Section 2
The Citizens of each State shall be entitled to all Privileges and Immunities of Citizens in the several States.

A Person charged in any State with Treason, Felony, or other Crime, who shall flee from Justice, and be found in another State, shall on demand of the executive Authority of the State from which he fled, be delivered up, to be removed to the State having Jurisdiction of the Crime.

No Person held to Service or Labour in one State, under the Laws thereof, escaping into another, shall, in Consequence of any Law or Regulation therein, be discharged from such Service or Labour, But shall be delivered up on Claim of the Party to whom such Service or Labour may be due.

Section 3
New States may be admitted by the Congress into this Union; but no new States shall be formed or erected within the Jurisdiction of any other State; nor any State be formed by the Junction of two or more States, or parts of States, without the Consent of the Legislatures of the States concerned as well as of the Congress.

The Congress shall have Power to dispose of and make all needful Rules and Regulations respecting the Territory or other Property belonging to the United States; and nothing in this Constitution shall be so construed as to Prejudice any Claims of the United States, or of any particular State.

Section 4
The United States shall guarantee to every State in this Union a Republican Form of Government, and shall protect each of them against Invasion; and on Application of the Legislature, or of the Executive (when the Legislature cannot be convened) against domestic Violence.

Article 5.

The Congress, whenever two thirds of both Houses shall deem it necessary, shall propose Amendments to this Constitution, or, on the Application of the Legislatures of two thirds of the several States, shall call a Convention for proposing Amendments, which, in either Case, shall be valid to all Intents and Purposes, as part of this Constitution, when ratified by the Legislatures of three fourths of the several States, or by Conventions in three fourths thereof, as the one or the other Mode of Ratification may be proposed by the Congress; Provided that no Amendment which may be made prior to the Year One thousand eight hundred and eight shall in any Manner affect the first and fourth Clauses in the Ninth Section of the first Article; and that no State, without its Consent, shall be deprived of its equal Suffrage in the Senate.

Article 6.

All Debts contracted and Engagements entered into, before the Adoption of this Constitution, shall be as valid against the United States under this Constitution, as under the Confederation.

This Constitution, and the Laws of the United States which shall be made in Pursuance thereof; and all Treaties made, or which shall be made, under the Authority of the United States, shall be the supreme Law of the Land; and the Judges in every State shall be bound thereby, any Thing in the Constitution or Laws of any State to the Contrary notwithstanding.

The Senators and Representatives before mentioned, and the Members of the several State Legislatures, and all executive and judicial Officers, both of the United States and of the several States, shall be bound by Oath or Affirmation, to support this Constitution; but no religious Test shall ever be required as a Qualification to any Office or public Trust under the United States.

Article 7.

The Ratification of the Conventions of nine States, shall be sufficient for the Establishment of this Constitution between the States so ratifying the Same.

Done in Convention by the Unanimous Consent of the States present the Seventeenth Day of September in the Year of our Lord one thousand seven hundred and Eighty seven and of the Independence of the United States of America the Twelfth. In Witness whereof We have hereunto subscribed our Names.

George Washington—President and deputy from Virginia

New Hampshire—John Langdon, Nicholas Gilman

Massachusetts—Nathaniel Gorham, Rufus King

Connecticut—William Samuel Johnson, Roger Sherman

New York—Alexander Hamilton

New Jersey—William Livingston, David Brearley, William Paterson, Jonathan Dayton

Pennsylvania—Benjamin Franklin, Thomas Mifflin, Robert Morris, George Clymer, Thomas Fitzsimons, Jared Ingersoll, James Wilson, Gouvernour Morris

Delaware—George Read, Gunning Bedford Jr., John Dickinson, Richard Bassett, Jacob Broom

Maryland   James McHenry, Daniel of St Thomas Jenifer, Daniel Carroll

Virginia—John Blair, James Madison Jr.

North Carolina—William Blount, Richard Dobbs Spaight, Hugh Williamson

South Carolina—John Rutledge, Charles Cotesworth Pinckney, Charles Pinckney, Pierce Butler

Georgia—William Few, Abraham Baldwin

Attest: William Jackson, Secretary

Amendment 1
Congress shall make no law respecting an establishment of religion, or prohibiting the free exercise thereof; or abridging the freedom of speech, or of the press; or the right of the people peaceably to assemble, and to petition the Government for a redress of grievances.

Amendment 2
A well regulated Militia, being necessary to the security of a free State, the right of the people to keep and bear Arms, shall not be infringed.

Amendment 3
No Soldier shall, in time of peace be quartered in any house, without the consent of the Owner, nor in time of war, but in a manner to be prescribed by law.

Amendment 4
The right of the people to be secure in their persons, houses, papers, and effects, against unreasonable searches and seizures, shall not be violated, and no Warrants shall issue, but upon probable cause, supported by Oath or affirmation, and particularly describing the place to be searched, and the persons or things to be seized.

Amendment 5
No person shall be held to answer for a capital, or otherwise infamous crime, unless on a presentment or indictment of a Grand Jury, except in cases arising in the land or naval forces, or in the Militia, when in actual service in time of War or public danger; nor shall any person be subject for the same offense to be twice put in jeopardy of life or limb; nor shall be compelled in any criminal case to be a witness against himself, nor be deprived of life, liberty, or property, without due process of law; nor shall private property be taken for public use, without just compensation.

Amendment 6
In all criminal prosecutions, the accused shall enjoy the right to a speedy and public trial, by an impartial jury of the State and district wherein the crime shall have been committed, which district shall have been previously ascertained by law, and to be informed of the nature and cause of the accusation; to be confronted with the witnesses against him; to have compulsory process for obtaining witnesses in his favor, and to have the Assistance of Counsel for his defence.

Amendment 7

In Suits at common law, where the value in controversy shall exceed twenty dollars, the right of trial by jury shall be preserved, and no fact tried by a jury, shall be otherwise re-examined in any Court of the United States, than according to the rules of the common law.

Amendment 8

Excessive bail shall not be required, nor excessive fines imposed, nor cruel and unusual punishments inflicted.

Amendment 9

The enumeration in the Constitution, of certain rights, shall not be construed to deny or disparage others retained by the people.

Amendment 10

The powers not delegated to the United States by the Constitution, nor prohibited by it to the States, are reserved to the States respectively, or to the people.

Amendment 11

The Judicial power of the United States shall not be construed to extend to any suit in law or equity, commenced or prosecuted against one of the United States by Citizens of another State, or by Citizens or Subjects of any Foreign State.

Amendment 12

The Electors shall meet in their respective states, and vote by ballot for President and Vice-President, one of whom, at least, shall not be an inhabitant of the same state with themselves; they shall name in their ballots the person voted for as President, and in distinct ballots the person voted for as Vice-President, and they shall make distinct lists of all persons voted for as President, and of all persons voted for as Vice-President and of the number of votes for each, which lists they shall sign and certify, and transmit sealed to the seat of the government of the United States, directed to the President of the Senate;

The President of the Senate shall, in the presence of the Senate and House of Representatives, open all the certificates and the votes shall then be counted;

The person having the greatest Number of votes for President, shall be the President, if such number be a majority of the whole number of Electors appointed; and if no person have such majority, then from the persons having the highest numbers not exceeding three on the list of those voted for as President, the House of Representatives shall choose immediately, by ballot, the President. But in choosing the President, the votes shall be taken by states, the representation from each state having one vote; a quorum for this purpose shall consist of a member or members from two-thirds of the states, and a majority of all the states shall be necessary to a choice. And if the House of Representatives shall not choose a President whenever the right of choice shall devolve upon them, before the fourth day of March next following, then the Vice-President shall act as President, as in the case of the death or other constitutional disability of the President.

The person having the greatest number of votes as Vice-President, shall be the Vice-President, if such number be a majority of the whole number of Electors appointed, and if no person have a majority, then from the two highest numbers on the list, the Senate shall choose the Vice-President; a quorum for the purpose shall consist of two-thirds of the whole number of Senators, and a majority of the whole number shall be necessary to a choice. But no person constitutionally ineligible to the office of President shall be eligible to that of Vice-President of the United States.

Amendment 13
1. Neither slavery nor involuntary servitude, except as a punishment for crime whereof the party shall have been duly convicted, shall exist within the United States, or any place subject to their jurisdiction.

2. Congress shall have power to enforce this article by appropriate legislation.

Amendment 14

1. All persons born or naturalized in the United States, and subject to the jurisdiction thereof, are citizens of the United States and of the State wherein they reside. No State shall make or enforce any law which shall abridge the privileges or immunities of citizens of the United States; nor shall any State deprive any person of life, liberty, or property, without due process of law; nor deny to any person within its jurisdiction the equal protection of the laws.

2. Representatives shall be apportioned among the several States according to their respective numbers, counting the whole number of persons in each State, excluding Indians not taxed. But when the right to vote at any election for the choice of electors for President and Vice-President of the United States, Representatives in Congress, the Executive and Judicial officers of a State, or the members of the Legislature thereof, is denied to any of the male inhabitants of such State, being twenty-one years of age, and citizens of the United States, or in any way abridged, except for participation in rebellion, or other crime, the basis of representation therein shall be reduced in the proportion which the number of such male citizens shall bear to the whole number of male citizens twenty-one years of age in such State.

3. No person shall be a Senator or Representative in Congress, or elector of President and Vice-President, or hold any office, civil or military, under the United States, or under any State, who, having previously taken an oath, as a member of Congress, or as an officer of the United States, or as a member of any State legislature, or as an executive or judicial officer of any State, to support the Constitution of the United States, shall have engaged in insurrection or rebellion against the same, or given aid or comfort to the enemies thereof. But Congress may by a vote of two-thirds of each House, remove such disability.

4. The validity of the public debt of the United States, authorized by law, including debts incurred for payment of pensions and bounties for services in suppressing insurrection or rebellion, shall not be questioned. But neither the United States nor any State shall

assume or pay any debt or obligation incurred in aid of insurrection or rebellion against the United States, or any claim for the loss or emancipation of any slave; but all such debts, obligations and claims shall be held illegal and void.

5. The Congress shall have power to enforce, by appropriate legislation, the provisions of this article.

Amendment 15
1. The right of citizens of the United States to vote shall not be denied or abridged by the United States or by any State on account of race, color, or previous condition of servitude.

2. The Congress shall have power to enforce this article by appropriate legislation.

Amendment 16
The Congress shall have power to lay and collect taxes on incomes, from whatever source derived, without apportionment among the several States, and without regard to any census or enumeration.

Amendment 17
The Senate of the United States shall be composed of two Senators from each State, elected by the people thereof, for six years; and each Senator shall have one vote. The electors in each State shall have the qualifications requisite for electors of the most numerous branch of the State legislatures.

When vacancies happen in the representation of any State in the Senate, the executive authority of such State shall issue writs of election to fill such vacancies: Provided, That the legislature of any State may empower the executive thereof to make temporary appointments until the people fill the vacancies by election as the legislature may direct.

This amendment shall not be so construed as to affect the election or term of any Senator chosen before it becomes valid as part of the Constitution.

Amendment 18
1. After one year from the ratification of this article the manufacture, sale, or transportation of intoxicating liquors within, the importation thereof into, or the exportation thereof from the United States and all territory subject to the jurisdiction thereof for beverage purposes is hereby prohibited.

2. The Congress and the several States shall have concurrent power to enforce this article by appropriate legislation.

3. This article shall be inoperative unless it shall have been ratified as an amendment to the Constitution by the legislatures of the several States, as provided in the Constitution, within seven years from the date of the submission hereof to the States by the Congress.

Amendment 19
The right of citizens of the United States to vote shall not be denied or abridged by the United States or by any State on account of sex.

Congress shall have power to enforce this article by appropriate legislation.

Amendment 20
1. The terms of the President and Vice President shall end at noon on the 20th day of January, and the terms of Senators and Representatives at noon on the 3d day of January, of the years in which such terms would have ended if this article had not been ratified; and the terms of their successors shall then begin.

2. The Congress shall assemble at least once in every year, and such meeting shall begin at noon on the 3d day of January, unless they shall by law appoint a different day.

3. If, at the time fixed for the beginning of the term of the President, the President elect shall have died, the Vice President elect shall become President. If a President shall not have been chosen before the time fixed for the beginning of his term, or if the President elect shall have failed to qualify, then the Vice President elect shall act as

President until a President shall have qualified; and the Congress may by law provide for the case wherein neither a President elect nor a Vice President elect shall have qualified, declaring who shall then act as President, or the manner in which one who is to act shall be selected, and such person shall act accordingly until a President or Vice President shall have qualified.

4. The Congress may by law provide for the case of the death of any of the persons from whom the House of Representatives may choose a President whenever the right of choice shall have devolved upon them, and for the case of the death of any of the persons from whom the Senate may choose a Vice President whenever the right of choice shall have devolved upon them.

5. Sections 1 and 2 shall take effect on the 15th day of October following the ratification of this article.

6. This article shall be inoperative unless it shall have been ratified as an amendment to the Constitution by the legislatures of three-fourths of the several States within seven years from the date of its submission.

Amendment 21
1. The eighteenth article of amendment to the Constitution of the United States is hereby repealed.

2. The transportation or importation into any State, Territory, or possession of the United States for delivery or use therein of intoxicating liquors, in violation of the laws thereof, is hereby prohibited.

3. The article shall be inoperative unless it shall have been ratified as an amendment to the Constitution by conventions in the several States, as provided in the Constitution, within seven years from the date of the submission hereof to the States by the Congress.

Amendment 22

1. No person shall be elected to the office of the President more than twice, and no person who has held the office of President, or acted as President, for more than two years of a term to which some other person was elected President shall be elected to the office of the President more than once. But this Article shall not apply to any person holding the office of President, when this Article was proposed by the Congress, and shall not prevent any person who may be holding the office of President, or acting as President, during the term within which this Article becomes operative from holding the office of President or acting as President during the remainder of such term.

2. This article shall be inoperative unless it shall have been ratified as an amendment to the Constitution by the legislatures of three-fourths of the several States within seven years from the date of its submission to the States by the Congress.

Amendment 23

1. The District constituting the seat of Government of the United States shall appoint in such manner as the Congress may direct: A number of electors of President and Vice President equal to the whole number of Senators and Representatives in Congress to which the District would be entitled if it were a State, but in no event more than the least populous State; they shall be in addition to those appointed by the States, but they shall be considered, for the purposes of the election of President and Vice President, to be electors appointed by a State; and they shall meet in the District and perform such duties as provided by the twelfth article of amendment.

2. The Congress shall have power to enforce this article by appropriate legislation.

Amendment 24

1. The right of citizens of the United States to vote in any primary or other election for President or Vice President, for electors for President or Vice President, or for Senator or Representative in

Congress, shall not be denied or abridged by the United States or any State by reason of failure to pay any poll tax or other tax.

2. The Congress shall have power to enforce this article by appropriate legislation.

Amendment 25
1. In case of the removal of the President from office or of his death or resignation, the Vice President shall become President.

2. Whenever there is a vacancy in the office of the Vice President, the President shall nominate a Vice President who shall take office upon confirmation by a majority vote of both Houses of Congress.

3. Whenever the President transmits to the President pro tempore of the Senate and the Speaker of the House of Representatives his written declaration that he is unable to discharge the powers and duties of his office, and until he transmits to them a written declaration to the contrary, such powers and duties shall be discharged by the Vice President as Acting President.

4. Whenever the Vice President and a majority of either the principal officers of the executive departments or of such other body as Congress may by law provide, transmit to the President pro tempore of the Senate and the Speaker of the House of Representatives their written declaration that the President is unable to discharge the powers and duties of his office, the Vice President shall immediately assume the powers and duties of the office as Acting President.

Thereafter, when the President transmits to the President pro tempore of the Senate and the Speaker of the House of Representatives his written declaration that no inability exists, he shall resume the powers and duties of his office unless the Vice President and a majority of either the principal officers of the executive department or of such other body as Congress may by law provide, transmit within four days to the President pro tempore of the Senate and the Speaker of the House of Representatives their written declaration that the President is unable to discharge the powers and duties of his office.

Thereupon Congress shall decide the issue, assembling within forty eight hours for that purpose if not in session. If the Congress, within twenty one days after receipt of the latter written declaration, or, if Congress is not in session, within twenty one days after Congress is required to assemble, determines by two thirds vote of both Houses that the President is unable to discharge the powers and duties of his office, the Vice President shall continue to discharge the same as Acting President; otherwise, the President shall resume the powers and duties of his office.

Amendment 26

1. The right of citizens of the United States, who are eighteen years of age or older, to vote shall not be denied or abridged by the United States or by any State on account of age.

2. The Congress shall have power to enforce this article by appropriate legislation.

Amendment 27

No law, varying the compensation for the services of the Senators and Representatives, shall take effect, until an election of Representatives shall have intervened.